C000142075

Homo loquens

Homo loquens

Man as a talking animal

DENNIS FRY

CAMBRIDGE UNIVERSITY PRESS
CAMBRIDGE
LONDON · NEW YORK · MELBOURNE

Published by the Syndics of the Cambridge University Press
The Pitt Building, Trumpington Street, Cambridge CB2 1RP
Bentley House, 200 Euston Road, London NW1 2DB
32 East 57th Street, New York, NY 10022, USA
296 Beaconsfield Parade, Middle Park, Melbourne 3206, Australia

First published 1977

Printed in Great Britain by
Cox & Wyman Ltd, London, Fakenham and Reading

Library of Congress Cataloguing in Publication Data

Fry, Dennis Butler.

Homo loquens.

1. Speech – Physiological aspects. I. Title.
QP306.F79 152.3′842 77–5134
ISBN 0 521 21705 9
ISBN 0 521 29239 5 pbk.

Contents

Preface

The following pages are addressed to that mythical creature 'the intelligent layman'. There seems to be no reason why some few thousands of words should not be added to the many millions that have been aimed at him in the past and there is at least this to be said with regard to the subject matter, that speech is an activity which the reader, whoever he may be, is pretty certain to be involved in for a considerable proportion of his waking life.

It will be abundantly clear to all those who are in the trade, who are of course equally intelligent but not laymen, that the information embodied in this book is culled from a thousand different sources and derived from a great many different people. The reason for not citing these in the text will be obvious enough: nothing is gained by loading the pages with a mass of names which have no previous associations for the majority of readers and will probably have been forgotten by them as soon as they have turned the page. The omission of references certainly does not imply any lack of gratitude on the part of the present author towards all those whose work in the past as well as at the present time provides the basis for what we know about speech and language. There is a Sechuana proverb which, translated as nearly as may be, says 'A man is not a man save with the help of others' and this is true with respect to any man's professional life just as it is in his physical, personal and social life. Whatever there may be of useful information or good sense in this book stems from a life-long contact with others working in this field. The names of an infinitely small proportion of them appear in the list of references given at the end of the book and I want to record my warmest thanks to these and to the many who are unnamed, all of whom have made the study of speech for me such a rewarding business.

1

Homo sapiens?

Speech is a mirror of the soul: as a man speaks, so is he.
Publius Syrus

Speech was given to the ordinary sort of men whereby to communicate their mind; but to wise men, whereby to conceal it.
Robert South

The label *homo sapiens* was first attached to man by Linnaeus in his classification of the animal kingdom over two hundred years ago. That kingdom is now thought to include over three-quarters of a million species, but no matter how many more may yet be discovered, it is unlikely that anything will ever seriously shake our conviction that we belong to a very special class, separated by an unbridgeable gulf from the rest of the animals, a conviction no less strong today than it was in the eighteenth century. The criteria on which Linnaeus's system was built were naturally physical in character but it is in the sphere of intelligence that man's superiority is generally reckoned to lie, whatever doubts one might occasionally have about the accuracy of the adjective *sapiens*.

The physiology of the human body parallels in a host of different ways that of the animals and even involves the working of a 'vegetative' system. Scientific research of recent years has in fact raised some doubt as to man's absolute monopoly of a number of traits which have always been viewed as lying within the realm of psychology; for example rats, if forced to exist in conditions of over-crowding and deprivation, may show all the signs of neurosis which have become familiar to us through observation of human behaviour; animals and even plants are said to 'suffer' on account of pain inflicted on some other organism and thus to exhibit the 'human' capacity for sympathy and altruism; moreover the progress made by a few individual chimpanzees in the use of sign language at least raises the question as to how far a rudimentary handling of language, as distinct from instinctual communication, may be accessible to some kinds of animal. Nonetheless man remains marked off from all the types of organism by which he is surrounded, mainly through the capacity which his brain provides for conceptualizing the world about him. Because man can think about and recall experiences which are not present in the here and now, because he can operate upon the concepts that result from these processes and can act upon his thinking, his relation with his environment is, as far as we know, unique.

It is not very likely that we shall ever be able finally to resolve the question whether the human ability to form concepts is the result of our learning to talk or whether acquiring language is a natural sequel to the forming of concepts. We can be sure that the two processes are closely linked to each other and that we should not be able to use language in the way that we do without developing conceptual thinking to an advanced stage. Man's particular position in organic life on earth must be attributed largely to his use of speech and language and to his capacity for both concrete and abstract thought. We stand in a rather special relation with all the things that we have a word for, we remember them differently, we think about them in a different way whether they stand for things like 'sofas' and 'signal-boxes' or like 'mortification' and 'Marxism'. The mental life of any individual who for one reason or another is prevented from acquiring language is vastly different from that of his fellow human beings.

But it is of course in the life of the human community rather than in that of the individual that speech and language play their major role. We can scarcely now imagine the condition of a human group totally lacking in any possibility of talk between its members. Talk means very much more than communication, for this we can observe going on among the birds and the bees; translated into human terms this would mean no more than the passing of information about a plentiful supply of nuts or the whereabouts of the next prey, the assertion of territorial rights or warning of the approach of the tribal enemy. A universe away from such matters is the variety of exchange represented by talk among people, with its myriad planes of intellectual, emotional and factual interchange which make up the infinitely complex web of social life. Without it human existence would be unrecognizably different.

Man is above everything else the talking animal – *homo loquens*. The overwhelming majority of human beings spend a great deal of their time talking and listening to each other. They learned to do so during the first few years of life – and without paying the process much overt attention – and in consequence the whole activity of speech communication is carried on at a level where neither speaker nor listener is very much aware of the mechanics of the business. We all of course have the illusion that we know what we are doing when we are talking, just as we have the illusion that we choose whether to speak or to be silent, although two minutes in a well-filled railway carriage should be enough to dispel the latter illusion. Because we talk and listen, we imagine that we know how speech works, yet the majority of us would not claim that we understand the circulation of the blood because blood flows in our veins, or oxygen exchange in the lungs because we breathe in and out. The situation with regard to speech is not very different and even from the technical point of view we are very far from knowing all there is to know about the operation of speech and language. Research into the diverse aspects of the subject has been going on now for many decades and has led to the establishing of a certain body of facts and general principles. This book is an attempt to make some of this information available to the ordinary reader, in the belief that it may be of interest and indeed of some importance to appreciate something of what it means to belong to the family of *homo loquens*.

2

Speech as brain-work

Within the book and volume of my brain. *Hamlet*

People talk for every imaginable reason. We talk to 'make friends and win people', as the advertisements used to say, and about equally often to make enemies and lose people; we may speak simply to impart knowledge but we speak also to influence, impress and persuade, to express our wants and to conceal them; above all, we speak to give tongue to our feelings, our love, admiration and sympathy, our anxiety, irritation or disgust. Small wonder that through the centuries writers have levelled a good deal more blame than praise at the tongue, that 'unruly member' which stands as the symbol for the whole machinery of human speech.

To use the word 'tongue' in this way is truly to employ a figure of speech. We may be aware that in speaking the tongue is wagging and certainly without its help articulate speech is all but impossible, yet talking is not all tongue-work any more than driving a car is simple hand- and foot-work. In all such human skills there lies behind the obvious working parts an immensely complex apparatus, much of it concerned with the control and the timing of the many actions that must go on. Important though the tongue is in speaking, it can do nothing except under instruction from the brain, so talking involves even more brain-work than tongue-work.

The brain of course plays a major role in the regulation of all our body functions and in the control of every kind of voluntary movement that we make. What makes speech a very special kind of activity from this point of view is the fact that it depends on the continual use of vast stores of information in our brain about the language we are using. All speech is based on knowledge of some given language, a fact which is recognized by the common use of the word 'tongue' to refer to language, as in our 'mother tongue', 'the tongues of men' and so on. It is literally the case that everyone who talks or listens carries round in his cortex an incredibly large stock of information about his mother tongue which he draws upon all the time he is talking or is taking in speech from other people. It is a commonplace that people can talk to each other only if they have a common language, but it is less immediately obvious what it means to have a language in common. In the simplest terms it means that two individuals who are in this position hold in their brain specific stores of language information which are so similar as to be in many respects identical. But what exactly do these stores consist of and how are they made use of when we are talking?

The simplest way to approach this question is through the language store we are most aware of – the store of words. Whenever we are talking our brain is busy selecting the words we need to convey our meaning and when someone is talking to us, we take in what they are saying in part by recognizing the words they use. To serve both these purposes, the brain contains an extensive dictionary of words to be found in our native language. Naturally the number of entries in this dictionary varies in individual brains and depends on the sort of upbringing and education the particular person has had, on the kind of job he does and on his personal tastes and tendencies. Some people have a decided taste for words, even a passion for them, and a few of these eventually become crossword or quiz champions or join Mensa. Others have quite noticeable difficulty in distinguishing between words that are at all alike in sound or spelling and are often not too clear as to how a particular word in the language is commonly used. In any case, the brain dictionary of an ordinary educated and literate person is likely to contain entries numbered in tens of thousands, perhaps twenty, thirty or forty thousand and maybe more. This large dictionary is made up of the words we are able to recognize when we hear them, words which we know the meaning and usage of at least in a general way. The large majority of these words are ones which we are all familiar with, so that individual brains carry a lot of word entries in common; indeed our dictionary would not be of much use if this were not the case and this factor constitutes a large part of what is meant by having a language in common. All the same each individual dictionary will contain some words not to be found in the dictionary of the next man, for A will be familiar with and recognize some words that B will not, so that if we were to pool all the words in all the individual brain dictionaries, we should have a collection which is not known in its entirety to any individual. It is this kind of list that is given in printed dictionaries; we should not expect to find anyone who could recognize all of the 75,000 words appearing in the Shorter Oxford English Dictionary.

Each of us has in his cortex then a dictionary containing some tens of thousands of words; but notice that these are the words we can recognize. When we ourselves talk, each of us uses a much smaller number of different words, just a few thousand, perhaps four to five at the most. To distinguish this much shorter list of words we might think of it as our 'active vocabulary' since it comprises all the words we are likely to utter when we are talking. The bigger dictionary of words we can recognize is our 'passive vocabulary'. Just as every individual has his own passive vocabulary, so each one will have a slightly different active vocabulary. One of the ways in which we build up our passive vocabulary is through having occasion to listen to a large number of different speakers and so getting to recognize the words that may turn up in the talk of any one of them.

All our lives we are learning new words and so adding to the dictionary entries in our brain. Right from our earliest years, these new words come into our passive vocabulary first, that is to say we learn to recognize them some time before we get round to using them in our own speech, if we ever do. Whenever some new and specialized field becomes a matter of public interest there is usually a group of words which gain particular currency and are for the general public new words. In recent years space travel has been one such area. We have all become familiar with words like 'astronaut', 'countdown' and 'module', first of all by hearing them on radio or television or by reading them in newspapers. In this way they have become part of our passive vocabulary; once they are familiar enough, they may well pass into our active vocabulary and be used in our conversation. Many of the entries in our dictionary get there through our reading and of these a considerable number are unlikely ever to appear in our active vocabulary.

The list of words that make up our personal dictionary is stored in a special part of our memory and although we do not realize that the dictionary is there, we are using it all the time. It is not at all clear to even the most advanced of present-day neurophysiologists exactly what the mechanism of memory is, but we can be fairly sure that in principle it is an arrangement of electrical circuits in the brain, so that the electronic computer probably does bear at least some resemblance to the human brain. A computer has a 'memory', where information is stowed away, and it has circuits which give access to the items of information when they are needed. Our everyday experience leaves us in no doubt that the brain is organized on this principle too, for we find only too often that we want to recover a word or a name and are quite unable to do so. This is not because the item is no longer in the dictionary, but because the circuits giving access to the entries are temporarily out of order. This must be the case because at some other moment, frequently when we stop searching for the word, it comes back to mind, proving that the dictionary entry was intact. As a matter of fact, access to our word dictionary works automatically and remarkably smoothly and reliably; the proportion of times when it lets us down is infinitesimally small compared with the millions and millions of operations which are successfully completed.

The most astonishing feature of the brain dictionary, and it shares this with other kinds of memory store, is the ease of access and the amazingly complex system of cross-referencing. When we use a printed dictionary, we have a technique for finding the word we want fairly efficiently by turning to the letter section, the page, the column and finally the word. But all this does take a certain time, no matter how practised we may be. The brain does it much more rapidly and automatically. Perhaps a good analogy can be seen in the way the brain deals with arithmetical operations. Those adults old enough to have had the invaluable experience of learning multiplication tables at school will know that if you have occasion to ask yourself what eight nines come to, the answer pops up in your brain like figures on a cash register; you certainly do not go serially through the eight times table. In a rather similar way you can recognize a word such as 'dromedary' without running through all the words beginning with *d* in your dictionary.

One of the reasons for this efficiency is that every item is cross-referenced in a hundred different ways. How often when we are trying to recall a word, and particularly a name, we are able to say 'It begins with *p*' or 'It begins with /sh/' (where we are thinking of the first sound and not the letters), or perhaps 'It ends in -ski'. Even more intriguing are the occasions when one says 'It's some name like Coleman' and it turns out to be perhaps 'Haskins'; we do not realize that the two names share trochaic rhythm, with a strong followed by a weaker syllable, and in this way they fall into the same class. Somewhere in our dictionary system the entries are card-indexed in this great variety of ways. When the brain is searching for some item, it does not rely on one method, as we do when we make use of the initial letter sequences in the printed dictionary, but applies all the possible criteria at the same time, checking the beginning, the middle and the ending of the word, its rhythmic pattern, and of course its associations and its meaning. It is partly by employing this technique of doing many operations in parallel that the brain achieves its vast superiority over man-made devices.

Your brain is equipped then with a very sizeable electronic dictionary and all the time someone is talking to you the access circuits are busy with the recognition of the words that are being said. When you yourself are talking, the brain is continuously selecting the words to convey what you want to say and these are found in the much smaller list forming your active vocabulary. From time to time it may of course dig around in the passive vocabulary and come up with a word which you very rarely use yourself or perhaps have never used before; it may well happen that you find yourself using it again after a short time so that it gradually enters firmly into your active vocabulary.

But words alone do not make a language and your brain stores many other kinds of information. Going to the dictionary of English words and pulling out a selection of them will not produce a very intelligible remark unless the words are placed in proper order, even if they all bear some relation to the subject you want to talk about. Here is a sentence in which all the words are quite appropriately chosen but are put together in random order:

> The half during child he if years every early interested it is passionately chance language given in a.

Your brain will have to do a great deal of work to make sense of this, certainly infinitely more work than it would do if the sentence were printed or spoken to you with the words in the right order. We shall see in a later chapter why it is possible for your brain to do the job at all.

In addition to the dictionary then the brain stores all the routines necessary for making up English sentences. It knows that 'Dog bites man' means one thing but that 'Man bites dog' means something quite different; that the sequence 'You have enough money' is appropriate when making a statement and 'Have you enough money' when asking a question, though the first can be a perfectly good question if you use the appropriate intonation while the second will never make a convincing English statement. The brain knows that 'You would never do that' will be readily understood but that 'Never you would do that', although readily understood will label the speaker as a non-native speaker of English. When we are speaking, the knowledge of all these routines and many more is called into play so that the structure of each remark shall be recognizable to anyone listening and shall get over what we wish to say without a great deal of confusion and error. As listeners we call upon this knowledge in order to follow the sense of what we hear.

The routines just referred to are clearly a formulation of the laws of grammar and syntax that apply to the language in question. In order to understand something of how speech works, it is necessary to digest the fact that every individual brain carries the formulation of these laws but that, as language users, we are unaware of possessing this knowledge and do not know explicitly what the laws are. It is, or at least was, true that during our schooldays we learned to make explicit the grammar and syntax of our native language. This is done through the medium of grammar books, generally, and a word or two must be said about the 'rules' they usually contain and their relation to the kind of grammar we are talking about here. First, the formulations given in grammar books almost invariably refer to a written language and this is not the same as the spoken language which we use when we are talking together. Second, grammar books are on the whole much concerned with the grammar which 'ought' to be used. The grammar book we carry in our brain, besides referring basically to the spoken language, formulates what we habitually do when we talk; it does not concern itself with what we 'should' or 'ought to' do, or with 'talking grammar', as they say. Any remark that is readily understood by listeners is grammatical, since the fact that it is understood shows that its grammar and syntax coincide with that familiar to the listeners. An example may help to make the point clear. In a Wiltshire village at about midday a group of children are playing in the main street; a woman comes to the door of a cottage and calls out something which seems to be a summons for some child or children to come to lunch. Whereupon one of the boys in the group exclaims: ''Er bain't a-callin' we, us don't belong to she'. This is a perfectly grammatical remark for it conforms exactly with the conventions of the language which is current among the children and is understood without the slightest hesitation. The grammatical usage is of course different from that current in other social groups and other versions of English where the subject and object cases of the personal pronouns would be reversed and the verb *to be* is conjugated with different forms instead of having the invariant form *be* in the affirmative and *bain't* in the negative. This does not alter the fact that the boy who spoke in this instance was making use of the grammatical and syntactic laws which he carried in his brain for his own language, and in fact was behaving exactly as we all do when we talk.

Word order or syntax is not the only aspect of grammar for which the brain holds the necessary routines. Just as sentences are formed from words placed in the right order, so words themselves are made up of grammatical segments technically referred to as *morphemes*. These are basically the roots of words together with the various particles which can be attached to beginning, middle or end of a root to denote some grammatical or semantic function. There is in English a fairly short list of morphemes which can be used only in conjunction with some other morpheme, things like *-ing*, which is linked to a verb stem in one form of the present tense, and *-s* and *-ed*, which also appear in verb forms, or *-er* and *-est*, which are attached to adjectives. Then there are morphemes like *un-* and *in-*, which denote negation, and *-less*, with similar function, or *-ness*, which converts an adjective into a noun, and *-ly*, which changes it into an adverb, all of which can occur only when linked to another morpheme. Many English word stems, on the other hand, can stand alone and so form single morpheme words like *wander, black, come, dictate,* etc. When we have occasion to use a word like *untrustworthy*, the brain has made use of the routines for building words from morphemes, in this instance no doubt by simply negating the adjective *trustworthy* with the morpheme *un-*, but the adjective itself is arrived at by attaching the noun *trust* to the adjective *worthy* which appears in other compounds such as *noteworthy, praiseworthy,* and so on. We make use all the time of multi-morpheme words like *easier, hopelessness, strikingly,* which are built up from the several morphemes rather than being listed complete in the brain dictionary. This not only effects some economy in storage but gives the freedom which is necessary for the formulating of the immense variety of sentences which we produce when talking and recognize when listening.

It might appear that with the morpheme we have got down

to the basic elements of the language but there is in fact one more level of operation at which the brain deals with speech. This can best be understood by considering a parallel with the written language. In this book we are of course concerned with the spoken language, what we might call the 'ear-language', but the 'eye-language' is derived from the spoken language and there are naturally many correspondences. Anything that appears in printed English is necessarily some arrangement of 26 letters and a space; these form the elementary signals of the eye-language. The ear-language too has its basic elements, referred to as the *phonemes* of the language, which are rather more numerous but function in the same sort of way. The alphabet forms a system in which every letter is distinct from every other; letters are strung together to form words and we cannot replace one letter by another or add to or take away from the string without changing the meaning of the word. Suppose that we begin with a string of four letters: *trap*; if we take away the first letter we at once have a word with a different meaning, *rap*; if we add *s* to the beginning of the word, again we get a different word, *strap*; further changes in the middle of the word will give *strip* or *strop* and of course there are plenty of changes which would convert the word into a meaningless sequence like *strog* or *strim*.

The phonemes of a language operate in an analogous way and in fact alphabetic writing is derived originally from the phonemic system, though in the case of English the two have diverged somewhat. The phonemes of English, like those of all other languages, form a system of units each one of which is distinct from every other; they are arranged in strings to make spoken words and, as with letters, it is not possible to replace one phoneme in a string by another without altering the meaning or destroying it altogether. They are differentiated from each other by the audible differences in the sounds which occur when people are talking, just as letters are differentiated by their shape, that is by visible differences. Since we are talking about sound differences, there is obviously some difficulty in carrying on the discussion in print and we have to rely on the alphabetic representation of these differences, but if you think of the sound of the following words: *pin, bin, tin, din, kin, thin, fin, sin, shin, win,* it is clear that it is the difference in the first sound that distinguishes them from each other. They are all different words and if we want to be understood in English, we cannot replace one of the initial sounds by another in a given context. Similar effects can be shown at other positions in the sequence, as in words like *rip, rib, writ, rid, rick, rig, rim, ring,* or *beat, bit, bet, bat, bought, boot, but, bait, boat* and so on. Within each group the difference in meaning is dependent on a difference in one phoneme and all the distinctions represented form part of the complete English phoneme system. Most English words differ from each other by more than one phoneme, just as printed words differ by more than one letter. We may have two words with no phoneme in common, like *stumps* and *handbag,* or with two common phonemes, like *stumps* and *humbug,* or three, like *humbug* and *handbag*. By examining enough spoken words, we shall in the end reach a point where the list of phonemes is complete and any fresh word does not involve an addition to it. In English this point is reached with an inventory of just over forty phonemes. Of these about twenty are the vowel phonemes, exemplified by the word group *beat, bit, bet, bat,* etc. It is here that the main divergences between English spelling and the phonemic system occur, since we have only five vowel letters and these have to be used in combination to represent the twenty vowel phonemes. This largely explains, by the way, why those interested in devising an alternative spelling to help children with reading difficulties generally have recourse to an alphabet of forty letters.

We have seen that there are differences of grammar between various versions of English and there are equally differences in the phonemic system. A speaker brought up in the south of England would have different vowel phonemes represented in the two parts of the word *sandcastle,* one brought up in the north would have the same vowel phoneme in both parts; again, a speaker brought up in Scotland would have two different consonant phonemes represented at the beginning of the words *where* and *wear,* or *which* and *witch,* the southern speaker only one. There are therefore small differences in the total number of phonemic units that make up the system in the different versions of English that are current.

It may not be obvious why we should not consider the phonemes to be simply the sounds of the language and why they should not be referred to in this way. Here again the analogy with the eye-language will be useful. Each of us produces our own individual version of the eye-language in the form of our handwriting. No two people write exactly alike and so the shape of a given letter varies from handwriting to handwriting. If we look closely at what is happening when we are reading someone's manuscript, we see that, although in a certain sense we are recognizing the shape of a letter, more precisely we are deciding that a given squiggle represents a given letter of the alphabet and not one of the other twenty-five. In other words, we are placing the mark on the paper in one of twenty-six classes by means of criteria which we carry in our brain. When people talk, the sounds which they make have at least as much variability as the letter-shapes they produce when they write and probably more. No two speakers make exactly the same sounds when they say the same words, and yet the brain of the listener recognizes each sound as belonging to one of the phonemes in the language system and in doing so he makes use of criteria which he carries in his brain. Later on we shall take a look at the part played by the ear in this process, for of course speech involves a lot of ear-work as well as tongue-work, but the important point is that phonemes are strictly language categories and they play an essential role in the processing of speech by the brain. In every individual brain is stored the complete list of phonemes for the language that is ordinarily used; when we have something to say, part of the process of saying it consists in arranging in the proper order the phoneme string that makes up the message, just as another part is the ordering of the words. For this purpose, we as English speakers call upon the phoneme system for our particular brand of English. When we are taking in speech, we have no difficulty in making the adjustments necessary to deal with a somewhat different type of English, just as we can understand someone who has a different grammar or a different vocabulary from our own. It is only when a speaker has a phonemic system very widely different from the one we use, for instance when he speaks an unfamiliar regional or national dialect, that we begin to experience real difficulty.

Languages differ from each other in their phoneme systems, just as they differ in grammar and vocabulary. Everyone appreciates that if he wants to learn a foreign language, he must acquire a vocabulary and learn a new grammar. Few people know or indeed are taught that learning a new language also means learning a new system of phonemes. This does not mean simply learning to pronounce some unaccustomed sounds, in the way that the Englishman learning French has to acquire a new vowel sound for use in words like *mur* and a set of nasalized vowels for *un bon vin blanc*. What the phoneme system does is to dictate for any language what particular sounds must be recognized as distinct from each other and what sound differences should be disregarded. English uses the difference between /s/ and /sh/ as a way of distinguishing words, so that we can find pairs like *save* and *shave, sin* and *shin, mass* and *mash*. The phonemic system of Dutch or of Spanish or of a number of Indian languages does not include this distinction and as a consequence native speakers of these languages are quite unable to perceive the difference in English unless they have made a special effort to learn to do so. This appears incredible to us because we believe of course that there is a self-evident and 'real' difference between the two sounds which must be obvious to everyone, but this is far from the truth. We distinguish the sounds because our phonemic system insists that we do so. Another example is to be found in the final sounds of *win* and *wing* which are indistinguishable to a native Italian speaker. This is all the more remarkable because an Italian does pronounce the final sound of *wing* in Italian words like *lungo, dunque, bianco*, but in all these cases it is followed by the sound of /g/ or /k/, as it is in the English word *sink*, and his language contains no pairs of words differentiated solely by the presence of either /n/ or /ng/. The phonemic system in quite a number of Indian languages includes as many as six different *t* sounds which are all but indistinguishable to the English ear. Among them is a pair which differ from each other in the same way as the *t* sounds in the two English words *tar* and *star*, but this is not a difference that has any function in the English system and we are therefore unaware of its existence. The functioning of a phonemic system is then much more a matter of how the brain organizes the acoustic information of speech than of the physical differences between sounds, though the latter has to be present in some degree as a basis for the perceptual organization. People who have a common language have learned to adopt a particular system and moving to another language means acquiring a new and additional system of phonemic organization.

So far we have seen that in order to deal with speech the brain stores information which includes a large dictionary of words, the routines for putting words together to make understandable sentences, the list of morphemes and the routines for assembling them into words, and the inventory of phonemes. Discussion of the last has brought us to the point of contact with the actual sounds of speech which we shall be considering in detail in a later chapter, but from the language point of view there remain two other aspects which we must look at in order to complete the picture. When we were talking about the various forms which a sentence could take, we noted that in English the same string of words could be converted from a statement into a question by changing the intonation, that is the inflection or tune of the utterance. The various intonations that can be given to a sentence are themselves part of the grammar of the spoken language and information about the intonation system is another component in the linguistic knowledge stored by the brain. As far as the sound of a message is concerned, the intonation is conveyed mainly by variations in pitch, quite literally the tune of a remark. Some of the tunes in the English intonation system can easily be exemplified by taking a single word and saying it in different ways. In the spoken language it often happens that just one word makes a complete sentence. Try saying aloud the word 'No', first of all as if replying to a question to which the answer is quite definitely 'No'; next say the word itself as a question, asking another person for confirmation that something really is not the case; then third, say the word 'No' again in answer to a question but implying 'not exactly' or 'but on the other hand'. You will now have produced three of the principal tunes that occur in the English intonation system, patterns that are readily recognized by English listeners as conveying the sense that has just been outlined. There are of course other tunes and more complex ones in English, and since most remarks consist of more than one word, they are usually spread out over a much longer string of phonemes, but the basic set of English intonation patterns is quite small and, again, is stored in the brain for use when sending out speech and when evaluating what other people say to us.

One further feature of speech which is closely bound up with the intonation is the rhythmic pattern. English is one of the languages in which any word said by itself will have one syllable which is relatively strongly stressed while others are weaker. In the word *table*, the first syllable is the strong one, the second the weaker; in *depart*, it is the other way round; *exciting* has the strong syllable in the middle with a weaker one on either side while *actually* has a first stressed syllable followed by weaker ones, and so on. Pairs of words do occur in English which are differentiated only by the rhythmic pattern or principally by this means. The word which is spelt *contract* in the eye-language may be a noun meaning something which is signed and then it has the strong syllable first, followed by a weaker one, or it may be a verb meaning to grow smaller, in which case the stress is on the second syllable. There are a considerable number of such pairs in English, among them *permit, object, rebel, import, export*. When words are strung together to make sentences of some length, the strong syllables tend to recur at more or less regular intervals with weaker syllables in between and it is this pattern that constitutes the characteristic rhythm of English speech. As a general rule the strong beat on a syllable of an English word is fixed and cannot be shifted when the word is embodied in a sentence, but those words which consist of one syllable only may account for a stronger or a weaker beat in the general pattern, depending upon their importance for the sense of the remark.

The pitch pattern and the rhythmic pattern of a spoken message are very intimately linked together. For example, the first tune which you used for the word 'No' above, a falling intonation, will tend to occur on the last strong syllable in a statement. Supposing you make some statement which ends with a reference to signing a contract, then this fall will take place in the syllable *con-* because this is the last strong syllable. If your statement, on the other hand, ended with the remark that something was beginning to contract, then the fall would be made in the syllable *-tract,* which is now the last strong syllable. It is by the combining of various features of the rhythm and intonation pattern that we convey to our hearers the relative importance of the different parts of any remark we make and that we make it clear to them whether we are asking a question or making a statement, issuing an order or making a polite request, whether we are in doubt about something or quite positive.

Different brands of English have different rhythm and intonation patterns just as they may have different vocabularies, grammars and phonemic systems. We have only to think of the characteristic intonations used by Scottish, Irish or Welsh speakers of English, or to imagine an American saying the word *interrogatory* to realize that the variations are very marked indeed, but again they do not generally prevent us from understanding what is said to us by speakers whose language background is different from our own.

It is not easy to visualize just how vast a store of information is represented by all this language knowledge but it is all indispensable to communication by speech and is literally present in the brain of every language-user, no matter what his mother tongue. The indications are that the storage space for the purpose is found in one particular part of the brain but there seems to be little likelihood that any individual will run out of language space. One estimate of the total storage capacity of the human brain puts this at 1000,000,000,000,000 items of information, and even though this refers to binary items it is still a stupendous capacity. For the majority of the people in the world the speech and language stores are occupied by the mother tongue; a much smaller number have added to this a second or third language. It is a somewhat sobering thought that those phenomenal beings who are said to speak six or ten languages have actually amassed information in their brain about vocabulary, syntax, grammar, phonemic system, intonation and rhythm patterns six or ten times over; they will certainly not possess the same degree of command over all of the systems but it is nonetheless an astounding achievement. It all depends, however, on that even more astonishing feat accomplished by every one of us less gifted mortals, the acquiring of our native language. When all is said and done, this remains the most brilliant achievement of the human brain.

3

Speech as tongue-work

> **Speak the speech, I pray you, as I pronounced it to you, trippingly on the tongue.**
> *Hamlet*

Speech communication means an interchange between at least two people. The linguistic knowledge which each of us carries in his brain forms the basis for this interchange and is a *sine qua non* for speech, but it would remain no more than a potential for communication if it were not externalized by means of the rest of the complex machinery for speech which we possess. The message formulated in the speaker's brain has to go through a number of transformations in order that it may eventually have some influence on the listener. What goes on in the speaker when he talks is essentially private in character and so, incidentally, is what goes on in the listener – which is often just as well from the point of view of personal relations. It is only by taking note of each other's behaviour, both visible and audible, that we can get some inkling as to whether our 'esteemed communication', as the secretarial schools have it, has been received, let alone understood. Fortunately each of us is both a speaker and a listener by turns and we become very adept at reading the signs which tell us whether what we say has been taken in. We communicate in a common language and this means, as we have seen, that the listener's brain carries substantially the same language information as the speaker's. The speaker's job is to set going a train of operations such that the sentences, the words, the morphemes and phonemes, the rhythm and intonation which constitute his message may be successfully inferred by the listener and we can say that communication is effective to the extent that the listener is able to do this.

Between the speaker's brain and the listener's there are three main links in the communication chain: the speech mechanism, the sound-waves in the air and the hearing mechanism. Anything that we say takes on a different form as it passes through these successive stages. We have seen that it sets out as a string of language elements of different kinds in the brain of the speaker. The speech mechanism, that is the complicated system of muscles we use when talking, converts these into a sequence of movements; the movements set up minute changes of pressure in the air, the sound-waves of speech, and these in turn impose movements on the hearing mechanism of anyone who is within earshot. The listener's brain uses the information transmitted by these movements to get back to the string of language elements that make up the message. We normally think of speech as being a unitary kind of activity but it is clear that it really consists of a series of changes or transformations. There is no way in which we can get over what we want to say to someone else without its undergoing this sequence of changes. An analogy which may perhaps help to make the point clearer can be seen by contrasting the letter and the telegram as methods of conveying a message to someone. When we send a letter, we write what we have to say on a sheet of paper and eventually, with any luck, the same sheet of paper lies before the eyes of the addressee who reads the marks that we originally made. A telegram, however, is a very different matter; we may go into a post office and write our message on a telegram form but this piece of paper will not of course be sent to the person we are addressing. Our message will be changed first into the movements of someone's fingers working a kind of typewriter, then into electrical pulses in a cable or perhaps modulating radio waves; at the receiving end the pulses will be changed into movements of a teleprinter or possibly be converted into spoken words sent along a telephone line. Communication by means of speech is analogous to the second method, that of a telegram with its many changes of form, and does not in any sense resemble the sending-a-letter method.

One thing that is immediately obvious is that as the message changes its form certain relations must be maintained between successive forms so that the contents of the message are not lost or seriously altered. In speech this means that there are correspondences between the language elements assembled in the speaker's brain, the speech movements which he makes, the resulting sound-waves, the movements in the listener's ear and finally the string of language units his brain arrives at. In succeeding chapters we shall take a look at the machinery we use to produce the various changes and the nature of the correspondences that are maintained between the different forms of the message.

Earlier on we noted that as far as the brain of the speaker is concerned the final form of the message is a string of phonemes with the appropriate rhythm and intonation pattern. The task of the muscular mechanism we use for speech is to convert the phoneme string into a sequence of movements, but before we go into the details of how this is done, there are a few general features of the speech mechanism that have to be taken into account. Speech, contrary to all appearances, is a form of work and the muscular speech mechanism is a piece of machinery for doing this physical work. Like all machines it has to get a supply of energy from somewhere; in the case of speech, the energy source is the lungs. This brings us to an important point about speech and that is that all the physiological apparatus we use for the purpose has more primary functions related to the job of simply keeping us alive. *Homo loquens* is a relatively late version of *homo* and a number of primary mechanisms have been pressed into service, as it were, to fulfil the secondary purpose of speech. We could live without talking but we certainly cannot talk without living. The primary purpose of the lungs is to maintain the oxygen exchange in the blood, a process which is kept going by breathing in air and exhaling carbon dioxide together with water vapour and small amounts of other gases. There may be some significance in the fact that the power for speech comes from exhalation only; the body makes sure of the supply of oxygen first and uses the act of getting rid of the waste products of breathing as the basis for speaking (speech is therefore literally, as well as often figuratively, 'hot air').

The rhythm of quiet breathing, that is to say when we are not talking, is generally a regular one though the frequency with which we take in breath varies with the circumstances. If you have just run upstairs or have run for a bus you will certainly be breathing in more often than you normally do when sitting quietly in an armchair. The average rate is something like fifteen breaths every minute, which means that one breath in and out takes four seconds. This time is divided more or less equally between the in and out part of the cycle. When we are talking, this regular breathing rhythm is drastically altered and for a very good reason. Since only exhalation provides the energy for speech and we can therefore talk only during the time when we are breathing out, if we kept to the regular breathing rhythm when we spoke, we should be silent for two seconds in every four, even when we wanted to talk continuously. Fortunately *homo loquens* has developed a very much more practical technique. When we take in breath in order to say something, we do so much more rapidly than in quiet breathing and we then use the breathing muscles to spin out the supply of air so that we can keep on speaking for much longer than the two seconds of exhalation that is common in quiet breathing. The time needed for breathing in can if necessary be cut down to something like a quarter of a second and the speech that follows can be extended to ten, fifteen or even twenty seconds. When we speak continuously, as we may do in reading aloud or in lecturing, or even sometimes in conversation, we repeat the pattern of a quick intake of breath succeeded by a long exhalation.

An interesting feature of speech breathing is that the moments at which we breathe in are far from being arranged haphazard; they are determined at the language level in the speaker's brain by the syntax of his remarks. You can check this easily by reading a couple of paragraphs aloud and noting the points at which you breathe in; you will find that they coincide with the end of a phrase, a clause or a sentence, depending on the pace at which you read and on the style of the writer. This effect is not confined to reading aloud, nor indeed to literate people. We do the same thing in conversation, for the brain when organizing the language form of the message is able to predict within reasonable limits the point at which the next breath can be taken and also the amount of air that needs to be taken in. This is so much the case that if we hesitate in order to find a word, we hold our breath so as not to break the link between the syntax of the message and the breathing pattern. If we talk fast, we simply opt for breathing points that are more widely spaced syntactically, and when we talk slowly we do the reverse.

It is quite possible to talk as breath is being taken in. Children often do this for fun and anyone can manage it with a few seconds' practice. It is not uncommon for an adult who is laughing heartily and continuously to make a sound as he draws in breath, as well as during exhalation, and this can prove rather trying for others. The speech mechanism will not however work very efficiently during inhalation; it is impossible to keep going for very long and the sound of the voice is very odd compared with that produced in the normal way.

Outgoing breath is then the power supply for speech. In order to generate the sound-waves of speech this power has to be applied to some device which will produce vibrations and this is found in the larynx, which is the basic sound source for speech. The channel for air entering and leaving the lungs leads from the two lungs into the windpipe, which runs up the front of the neck and ends in the rather curiously shaped structure which we know as the Adam's apple. This is the thyroid cartilage which can be readily seen or felt with the thumb and forefinger in the front of the neck under the chin. The cartilage is made up of two plates roughly in the shape of a shield (hence the name given to it), joined together in the front and with a small notch at the top. Inside this protective structure there is a very complicated assembly of cartilages and muscles which make up the larynx mechanism. Among these is a pair of small muscles which run horizontally from the inside of the thyroid cartilage towards the back wall of the throat. Each of the muscles is edged by a whitish ligament and these edges are the vocal cords. During quiet breathing, that is when we are not talking, there is a more or less triangular space between the vocal cords because the front ends are attached to the thyroid close to each other, while the back ends are separated. While the cords are in this position, air can pass freely between them without generating any sound. There are other muscles and cartilages in the larynx by means of which the back ends of the vocal cords can be brought together and held so that the two cords are touching along their whole length. The effect of this action is to interpose, as it were, a shelf across the airway leading from the lungs to the mouth and so provide an entry valve to the chest. Here we see the primary function of the larynx mechanism, for closing the valve by bringing the cords firmly together prevents the entry of any dangerous substance into the lungs and also makes it possible for the chest to offer the resistance necessary when lifting a heavy weight with the arms or when bearing down.

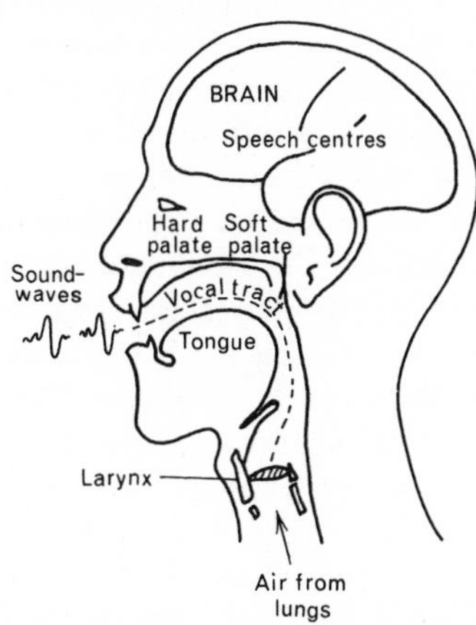

The action of the vocal cords in speech is however somewhat different. During speech air is flowing continuously outwards from the lungs. The cords are brought together and thus present an obstacle to the flow of air, with the result that the air pressure on the lower surface of the cords rises. When this increase of pressure reaches a certain level, the closed cords are no longer able to withstand the force of the air and they part from each other, allowing a puff of air to escape upwards. As soon as this happens, air pressure below the cords drops and the cords close together again, partly because of their own elasticity and partly because of a suction effect which develops on the underside of the cords. At this point the same cycle of physical effects recurs, with a rise of pressure below the cords and its release in a puff of air. The continued repetition of the cycle of vocal cord movement results in a stream of puffs or pulses of air and these constitute the basic vibrations of speech, the sound of voice. The vibratory effect of vocal cord movement can easily be felt by placing the thumb and forefinger on either side of the Adam's apple and saying a vigorous and prolonged *zzz* . . .

The operation of all the laryngeal muscles, and hence of the action of the vocal cords, is under voluntary control and during speech the brain regulates larynx action in the finest degree. The length of the vocal cords, their tension, their shape and the amount of contact between them are all controlled by the force exerted by the various muscles. The brain continually adjusts these forces in such a way as to alter the time interval between successive pulses of air. When the interval is long, the pitch of the sound is low, and as it grows shorter, the pitch rises. The average interval for men's voices is about eight thousandths of a second (8 milliseconds) or a frequency of 120 cycles per second. This corresponds to a note on the piano which is about an octave and a semitone below middle C. The average for women's speaking voices is not quite an octave above this and is in the region of 220 cycles per second, about three semitones below middle C, with an interval between larynx pulses of about 4·5 milliseconds. Both men and women when talking produce some very low-pitched and irregular vibrations of the vocal cords at the end of certain utterances and the time between one pulse and the next may become as long as 30 milliseconds, a frequency of 32 cycles per second.

Vibration of the vocal cords produces the sound referred to as 'voice' which is the basis of both singing and speaking. During singing, the larynx frequency remains steady for the length of each musical note whereas in speech the pitch of the larynx note changes all the time; it slides up and down continuously. The intonation patterns mentioned when we were discussing the language organization of the spoken message are reflected in the speech sounds mainly in the varying pitch of the larynx vibrations. Here we encounter the first of the correspondences between linguistic form and the action of the speech mechanism. In order to produce the first version of the word 'No', the definite statement (see p. 17), your brain had to instruct your larynx muscles in such a way that when you began the word the pitch of the larynx tone was relatively high and then to adjust the force of the larynx muscles continuously to bring about a sliding down of the pitch until at the end of the word the pitch was very low. For the second version, the question intonation, the general direction of the pitch change was the reverse, from low to high but using a different part of your voice range, probably beginning towards the middle. In the third intonation, the one implying doubt or meaning that there is more to say, the two directions are combined, a slide down being followed by a slide up in pitch. We begin to see what a tremendously complicated job the brain is doing in instructing the muscles of the speech mechanism when the language form of the message is being converted into movements. Usually when we talk the stretches of speech are much longer and require more complex intonation patterns; throughout them all the brain exerts control of the moment to moment changes in the adjustment of the larynx muscles, ensuring that the time interval between pulses of air from the larynx is now longer, now shorter so that the pitch patterns are appropriate to the intonation that the language and the circumstances demand.

From the language point of view the larynx mechanism has another very important function. By making a prolonged *zzz . . .* you were able to feel the effect of the larynx vibrations. If you try making a prolonged *sss . . .* you will find that these vibrations cannot now be felt; for this sound the vocal cords are not brought together and made to vibrate, but are held in the separated position, leaving the triangular space between them more or less as in quiet breathing. Although vibration of the vocal cords is the basic sound source for speech, all language systems require that at certain times in the stream of speech the vibratory mechanism shall be switched off. If we compare the two words *buzzing* and *hissing*, we find that in the first vibration continues through the middle of the word but in the second it has to be switched off for a short time. In English there are nine sounds for which the larynx vibrations are regularly switched off when the corresponding phonemes occur in the phoneme string; they are /p/, /t/, /k/, /ch/, /f/, /th/ (in *thin* but not in *then*), /s/, /sh/ and /h/. Among the instructions that go from the brain to the larynx all the time you are talking is one which switches the vocal cords from the vibrating to the open position whenever any one of these phonemes turns up in the message.

Before we leave the larynx mechanism, there are two more general functions which it fulfils and which we might refer to briefly. The question of how loudly we talk at any time is not on the whole very closely bound up with language; it is much more dependent upon the circumstances of the moment – where we are talking, whom we are talking to, what we are talking about and, most important of all, how much noise there is around us. We do like to talk to ourselves, not in the sense in which we say that so-and-so 'loves the sound of his own voice', nor in the way that people behave when they begin putting straws in their hair, as the saying goes, but as a matter of physical necessity we need a certain margin of difference between the loudness of our own speech and that of any noise in the background. When we are surrounded by noise therefore we raise our voice so as to try to achieve this desirable margin. This is in fact the real cocktail party problem. When you have thirty people in a room, a good three-quarters of whom are talking at the same time, every individual wants to keep a suitable difference between his own voice and the background, but unfortunately this background is provided by other people who want to do the same thing, and so we enter a vicious circle of what we might call noise inflation. The exhaustion that most of us feel after a cocktail party is not entirely attributable to the alcohol.

This variation in the loudness of our speech is mainly a

function of the larynx because it depends on the size of the puffs of air coming from the vocal cords. Certain adjustments of the larynx muscles result in a greater flow of air with each puff and hence in a louder voice sound, and this is why we tend to feel the cocktail party effect in the throat (as well as in the head). Air-flow is of course dependent also on the supply of air from the lungs and this can be increased by the chest muscles; if you shout very loudly, you may be able to feel a certain effort in the chest as well as in the throat.

The whole time we are talking the brain is monitoring the relations of loudness between background noise and speech and instructing the chest and larynx muscles accordingly. It is also taking care of much shorter term variations in loudness which are in fact related to the language aspect of speech. The rhythmic pattern which we spoke about earlier, the difference between stronger and weaker syllables, does involve a component of loudness. The middle syllable of *excitement* is louder than the one on either side of it, though there are other differences too, so larynx action has to be controlled by the brain, not only with regard to the frequency of the vocal cord vibrations, but also with respect to their strength.

Finally, the action of the larynx is responsible for what we generally refer to as the 'tone of voice' which a speaker uses. This is bound up with the emotional attitude of the speaker towards the situation, the person he is talking to and the subject, rather than the strictly linguistic side of the message, though the choice of words is naturally very closely linked with this affective aspect. The tone of voice which is appropriate for 'Darling I love you' will scarcely do for 'You filthy swine', or indeed vice versa. The enormously wide range of emotional tones available in speech running, not from A to B, as Dorothy Parker cruelly remarked of the well-known actress, but from A to Z, from admiration, aggression, awe and anxiety through disgust, envy, joy and love to pleasure, suspicion, triumph and zest, are all the work of the larynx mechanism which is on the whole the most primitive part of the speech mechanism. Wherever these emotions originate in us, as far as speech is concerned they are mediated by the brain and come out in our tone of voice which is the result of varying laryngeal adjustments.

The sound source for most of the time in speech is then the vibration of the vocal cords; this supplies the carrier wave, as it were, which makes our speech audible even over a certain distance and in competition with noise. The sound generated at the larynx also carries a proportion of language information, concerning intonation and rhythm and, to a small extent, the phoneme system insofar as this calls for the switching on and off of larynx vibration. Essential as these components are in the stream of speech, they do not by themselves serve to convey a great deal of language information. You can check this easily by making some remark while keeping your lips closed. The result will be a more or less continuous modified *mmm . . .* sort of sound. Anyone listening to you will be able to appreciate the intonation and rhythm of what you are saying, and even perhaps your tone of voice, but he will have no idea what you mean to convey because he is lacking the phonemic information which enables us to understand, to decode the message. We must now turn, therefore, to the means by which the brain imposes upon the stream of speech sound variations which transmit this information.

The channel for exhaled air which leads from the lungs through the windpipe to the larynx continues upwards through the pharynx, that is the space behind the tongue, into the mouth and out through the lips. There is a side branch to this channel which leads up at the back of the mouth into the nose and out through the nostrils. This system of air pathways from the larynx outwards is referred to as the *vocal tract* and it is here that the movements are made which convert the carrier wave from the larynx into articulate speech. This mechanism too has a primary function in the chewing and swallowing of the food which is indispensable for keeping us alive. The muscles of the pharynx, the tongue, the soft palate and the lips all take part in the process of articulation which depends on continual changes in the shape of the vocal tract, and hence in its acoustic properties. The first major effect of articulation is to shape the stream of sound coming from the larynx into a succession of syllables. If the vocal tract is narrowed down rather drastically at any point, the volume of sound issuing from the mouth is reduced. When the vocal tract is fairly well open along its whole length, on the other hand, the volume is high. Each syllable consists of a short stretch with the tract relatively open, preceded and followed by a period when the tract is narrowed and the volume of sound decreased. The effect is somewhat analogous to that of the swell-box of an organ or to the 'wa-wa' effect that jazz musicians used to produce by waving a bowler hat over the bell of a trombone, a trick that was resorted to incidentally to give the illusion of articulated sound coming from the instrument.

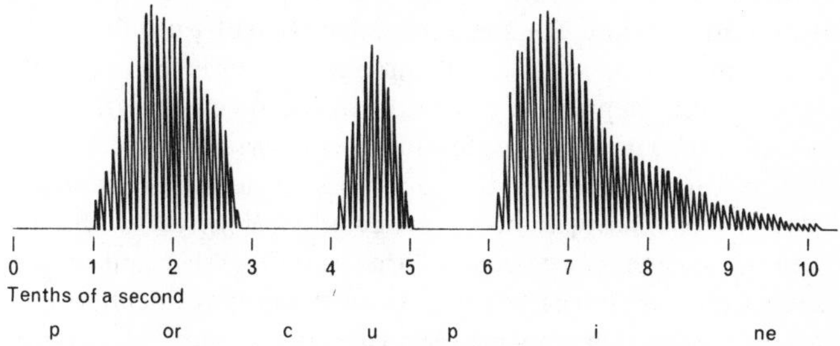

Each syllable in speech requires a stretch of high amplitude vibrations from the larynx. The three bursts of larynx activity for the word *porcupine* are shown schematically here. Larynx vibration is switched off for voiceless sounds, like the initial *p*, the *c* and the second *p* in this word, but is maintained for voiced sounds, the three vowels and the final *n*. The whole word lasts about one second and the larynx is vibrating for approximately 70 per cent of this time.

The open-tract parts of the syllables correspond to the vowel phonemes in the phoneme system. In an English word like *porcupine* there are three syllables and therefore three periods when the vocal tract is relatively open; these are separated by articulatory movements which close down the tract. At the beginning of the word this is done by bringing the two lips together, after the first syllable by shutting off the back of the mouth with the back of the tongue, after the second syllable by closing the lips again and finally by closing the mouth with the front of the tongue along the gums of the upper teeth. The closing movements correspond to the consonant phonemes in the phoneme string and the general scheme is one of alternations of consonant and vowel phonemes signalled by alternating closing and opening movements of the tract. Most of the consonant articulations are performed by the tongue or the lips, with some help from the soft palate. For much of the time during speech the soft palate is held raised by the muscles attached to it so as to shut off the side branch of the vocal tract which leads out through the nose. In articulating nasal sounds, however, like the final *n* of *porcupine*, the soft palate comes to its lowered, resting position thus opening the air passage through the nose while the mouth passage is closed by the front of the tongue. For some consonant articulations the vocal tract is momentarily sealed off completely; this is the case with /p, t, k/ for example. In others the air passage is greatly narrowed without being quite closed, and when air is forced rapidly through the narrow gap a hissing noise is generated. This is what happens in the articulation of /f, th, s, sh/. In running speech many syllables are strung together and we do not get regular alternation of one vowel, one consonant articulation; we may get consonants clustering together even in one syllable, as in a word like *straight* and we may also get cases in which a vowel begins or ends the utterance. If we exclaim 'Oh!' for example, this is a syllable in which the consonant articulation both before and after the vowel is replaced by silence, the extreme case of low volume sound from the vocal tract.

Earlier on we had examples of vowel phonemes in the series of words *beat, bit, bet, bat,* etc. All vowel articulations require the vocal tract to be relatively open but the extent of this opening differs for different vowels. For *beat* and *boot* the air passage through the mouth is shaped into a relatively narrow channel, the difference between the two being that the narrowing is made in the front of the mouth for *beat* and at the back, under the soft palate, for *boot*. For the vowel of *bard*, on the other hand, the air channel through the mouth is really wide open. As we shall see in the next chapter, the importance of

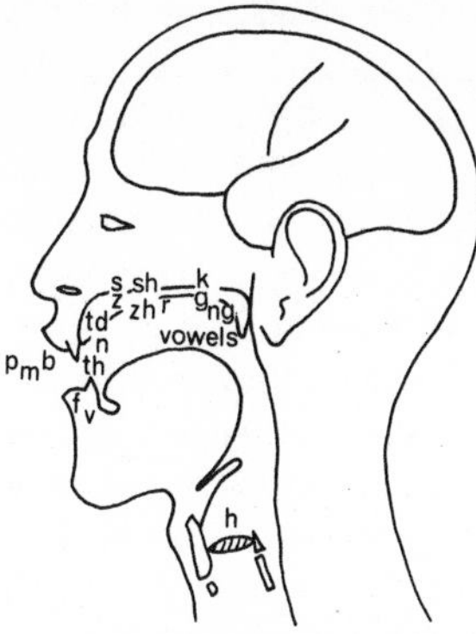

The various sounds of English are made at different places in the vocal tract and these are shown approximately by the positions of the letters.

these modifications in the shape of the vocal tract is that they alter the resonances of the whole acoustic system and give rise to sounds which we hear as having different qualities or colours which we have learned to associate with the various vowel phonemes. For certain of the phonemes the sounds involve a noticeable shift of colour within one syllable; this is the case in *bait, boat, bite* and *bout*. This type of sound and the phoneme with which it is associated is referred to as a diphthong.

For all the vowel sounds and for a majority of the consonants the larynx mechanism is kept in vibration but we noted earlier that in English there are nine consonants for which the vocal cord vibration is switched off. This does not mean of course that no sound is associated with these consonants but rather that during their articulation the sound of voice from the larynx is replaced by a noise. The noises are produced by forcing air rapidly through a narrow gap and they can be generated at many places along the vocal tract by shifting the point at which the narrow gap is set up. The first sound in the word *fin* is a noise produced by making a narrow opening between the upper front teeth and the lower lip; in *thin,* the gap is between the tongue tip and the upper teeth, in *sin,* between the tongue tip (or for some people the blade of the tongue) and the gums of the upper teeth and in *shin*, between the blade of the tongue and a point just behind the gums of the upper teeth. For the first sound in *him*, the noise is generated actually at the larynx by forcing air between the vocal cords without making them vibrate. It is clear then that the place where the noise is produced has an effect on the kind of noise we hear and we rely on these differences in distinguishing the sounds that represent the various consonant phonemes, just as different vowel sounds are characterized by their place of articulation.

One particular type of consonant articulation gives rise to noise in a slightly different way. All the time we are talking air is flowing out from the lungs; if the vocal tract is shut off completely at any point, then air pressure will build up behind the closure and a sudden opening of the obstruction will produce a short explosive noise. This is the method used for the /p, t, k/ group already mentioned and again it is evident that the place where the closure is effected determines the quality of the sound. In /p/ the closure is made by the two lips, in /t/, by the front of the tongue against the gums of the upper teeth and in /k/, by the back of the tongue against the soft palate and each makes its characteristic little burst of noise. Whenever the closure occurs in the stream of speech sound, this interposes a very short silence; strange though it may seem, the way in which this silence begins is itself indicative of the place where the sound is being made. There are many instances in which /p, t, k/ are represented solely by this silence, for example when any of them occurs right at the end of a remark or when two of them occur in succession; in the latter case there will generally be a burst of noise only for the second consonant. If you say aloud the word *cocktail*, you will almost certainly find that /t/ has its burst of explosive noise but that /k/ is represented simply by its own particular brand of silence.

A final point about the noises that occur in speech is that some of them require the larynx sound source to be working as well as the noise source. The sounds during which the larynx is switched off are called *voiceless* and there is a tendency in language systems for voiceless consonants to have counterparts in which noise is produced at the same place in the vocal tract but larynx vibration is going on at the same time. This is the case for eight of the English voiceless consonants. Thus /p, t, k/ have corresponding *voiced* sounds /b, d, g/; the voiceless /ch/ has a voiced counterpart heard in the middle of the word *ledger*, and the continuous noises occur with vocal cord vibration in the words *liver, mother, wiser* and *leisure*.

The phonemic distinctions which are of such fundamental importance for language structure are reflected in the realm of articulation in an extremely complicated way. Although larynx action makes some contribution, as we have just seen, the major role is played by the tongue and it is no accident that the latter has become very much identified with speech and even with language. The soft palate is also an important component in the speech mechanism because for most of the time in speech it is necessary for the air passage to the nose to be shut off. In the articulation of the nasal consonants /m, n, ng/, however, this passage has to remain open and it is the mouth branch of the vocal tract which is closed off; for /m/ this is done at the same place as for /p, b/, for /n/, at the point for /t,

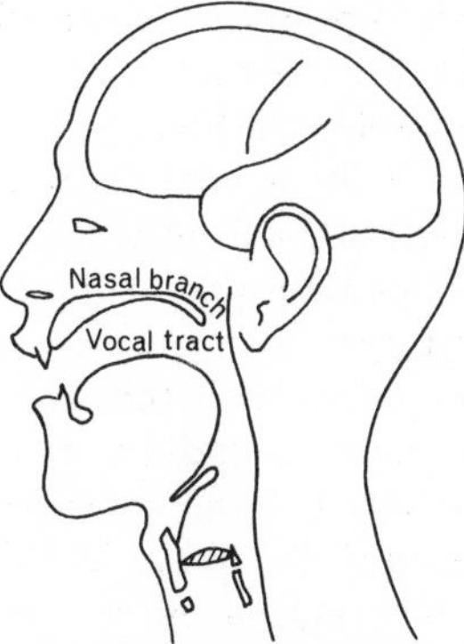

The vocal tract with the soft palate lowered and the nasal branch open as it is in quiet breathing and in producing /m, n, ng/ or nasal vowels like those in the French phrase *un bon vin blanc*.

d/ and for /ng/, at the point for /k, g/. This explains why a heavy head cold, which causes an obstruction of the nose, tends to make our nasal consonants sound like /b/, /d/ and /g/. The soft palate can contribute to articulation in various ways in different languages. The vowels in the French expression *un bon vin blanc,* require the speaker to articulate a vowel in the mouth in the normal way but to keep the air passage through the nose open at the same time.

The lips also have a share in articulatory activity, though it tends to be a somewhat secondary one. In languages generally there is some tendency for certain types of tongue movement to be accomplished by particular lip gestures. This is not surprising since all parts of the speech mechanism are linked together and a move in one place must produce a reaction in other sections of the vocal tract. Vowel sounds which entail a tongue movement towards the front of the mouth, for example, usually result in the lips being spread lengthwise as in smiling. This explains why people are constantly being enjoined to 'cheese' in front of the camera. A movement of the tongue to the back of the mouth, on the other hand, leads to a rounding of the lips into something like the position for whistling. English on the whole is in step with these natural trends; you will find it, for example, virtually impossible to pronounce the word *wood* with your lips in a fully spread position. In other languages, however, there are articulations which go against these trends. The vowel in the French word *pur,* for instance, gives the greatest difficulty to English speakers because it calls for a vowel made well to the front of the mouth but with the rounded lips which we find quite natural in the word *wood,* and it takes a great deal of practice for the Englishman to achieve these two requirements at the same time. The Japanese system, on the other hand, includes a vowel made at the back of the mouth, somewhat like the vowel in the English word *hood,* but with the lips fully spread as for *cheese,* a difficult combination for most non-Japanese speakers.

To transpose into the articulatory sphere all the distinctions carried by the phonemic system and to maintain the necessary correspondences so that the message can eventually be understood necessitates the working of all this complex machinery made up of the breathing muscles, the larynx muscles, the pharynx, the tongue, the soft palate, the lips, working as a co-ordinated whole under instructions from the brain. How the control is achieved will be the subject of a later section. It may be useful meanwhile, by way of a summary of the operation of the articulatory system, to give a blow-by-blow account, necessarily very much simplified, of the actions carried out in the course of quite a short remark in English. Imagine that you have to say to someone: 'I don't think I can'. What exactly is going to happen in your speech mechanism?

First, you will take in a rapid breath, not too much air because the whole remark involves only five syllables and the brain knows from long experience how much this requires and has already planned an utterance with just five relatively high-volume stretches of sound. The first syllable begins straight away with a vowel, so the vocal cord vibrations are switched on immediately as the tongue moves to a place somewhat more than halfway back in the mouth space and very low down. At the same time, or rather by the moment at which the cords begin vibrating, the soft palate is lifted to shut off the nasal passage. The tongue then moves rather slowly forward and up in the mouth to about where it would be if you were saying *it*. The next move is a very rapid one; the tongue makes itself very flat and spreads out sideways so that its edge is clamped against the gums of the upper teeth all the way round, so that there is an air seal. This is the first part of the /d/ articulation; it does not result in complete silence because the vocal cords are still vibrating. After a short time the tongue is drawn smartly away from its contact with the gums and bunches itself in the middle of the mouth space to start the vowel of *don't*. This, like the vowel of *I*, is a diphthong so there is a slow move, backwards and upwards this time, to complete the vowel or open tract section of the second syllable.

The next manoeuvre is a complicated one and introduces a new aspect of the brain's control of articulation. It has to arrange the articulation of /n/, /t/ and /th/ before the next vowel comes along and since everything is planned in advance, it is able to reduce the amount of movement so long as this does not create any difficulty in understanding the message. The /n/ and /t/ would most often be made with the tongue against the gums of the upper teeth, but the /th/ will need the air gap to be made farther forward at the teeth themselves. The brain foresees this and knows that if /n/ and /t/ are made at the same place as /th/, no one will ever know the difference. After the vowel of *don't*, therefore, the tongue flattens and spreads itself but this time to make contact all round against the upper teeth, not the gums, and in perfect synchrony the soft palate drops so that the air passage through the nose is opened just as the mouth passage is closed. This condition is maintained for an appreciable time and then there is a swift move of the soft palate upwards to close the nose passage and the vocal cord vibration is switched off at exactly the same moment, the tongue remaining still in close contact with the teeth. Now that both branches of the vocal tract are closed, by the soft palate and the tongue, pressure builds up in the mouth while there is a short silence in the stream of sound. The release of this pressure comes with quite a small movement of the tongue which brings the blade away from its contact with the teeth in the middle and opens a small gap through which is forced the air contained in the mouth and the pharynx. The short burst of noise which /t/ would normally occasion is therefore absorbed in the relatively faint hissing sound of /th/. The vocal cord vibrations are then switched on again while the tongue bunches well to the front of the mouth for the vowel of *think*.

The next articulation is for /ng/, since the word *think* is pronounced like the word *thing* with /k/ added to it. For this the mouth passage is closed by raising the back of the tongue against the soft palate while the nasal passage is opened by lowering the soft palate. After the /ng/ there is no move of the tongue which is already in position for /k/, but the soft palate is raised to shut off the nasal passage and the larynx vibrations are switched off. The short silence is followed by a little burst of noise for /k/ and then the larynx is switched on again and the tongue moves down to the floor of the mouth for the first part of the diphthong in *I*. Again there is the slow move up and forward for the second part of the diphthong and then the tongue moves rapidly back to make complete contact with the soft palate to build up the pressure for /k/, with the vocal cords switched off once more. A small explosive noise signals the release of pressure for /k/ and the tongue then flattens and lies fairly well forward for the vowel of *can*, larynx vibration being now switched on again. Finally the tongue spreads and rises to make contact this time with the gums of the upper teeth all round and the soft palate drops to leave the passage through the nose open.

Throughout all this complicated activity the action of the larynx is also being controlled to give the appropriate variations in frequency to convey the intonation pattern. It happens that there are at least five possible versions from this point of view since any one of the syllables in turn can be specially emphasized: *I* don't think I can; I *don't* think I can, etc., etc. If we select the most neutral version, a plain statement of fact, then the greatest volume of sound will probably be on *don't* and *can*, with the highest voice pitch on *don't* and the word *can* beginning on some mid-frequency and sliding down to the very lowest frequency at the end.

It must be underlined that this description of articulatory activity is enormously simplified; there is a great deal more going on that cannot be given in detail. One's first reaction perhaps is amazement that we have the persistence to carry on with it and we should certainly not do so but for the fact that we operate the whole machinery without paying it any attention. We are able to do so simply because we learned the skill in our very early years and ever since have been able to run it as automatically as we do many other motor activities. We shall see in a later chapter something of what is involved in the learning. We can only be thankful that man, if he is going to talk, can do so in such an effortless way, though on reflection it might be rather a good thing if we did have to pay a somewhat higher price for a unique gift.

4

Speech as sound-waves

The sound must seem an echo to the sense. Alexander Pope

Translating a spoken message out of the language form in which it is conceived by the speaker's brain into the articulatory form that we have just been considering obviously introduces a great deal of complexity and variability into the communication process. The inventory of phonemes, to take only one level of the language formulation, is now represented by patterns of activity on the part of a vast number of different muscles, patterns which vary in some measure with the particular sequence of movements and which certainly differ widely when produced by different individual speakers. Since we know that speech communication works, we know that the articulatory version of a message must embody the kind of correspondences with the language form that are needed for the ultimate understanding, or at least the decoding, of what has been said. After all the articulatory activity, however, the message is still in a 'private' form, one personal to the speaker. It is only because the speaker's movements give rise to sound-waves that the content of the message becomes publicly available. In this chapter we shall look at the speech mechanism as a generator of sound-waves and see what are its important properties from this point of view and what are the special features of speech sound-waves regarded as a medium for the language system.

The receiving apparatus for speech is the ear and brain and the most important property of sound-waves in general is that they provide a suitable input for this receiver, they are in some sense matched to the hearing mechanism. The ear is a device which registers very small changes of pressure in the air which surrounds it. Living on earth we are subjected to some relatively large changes in air pressure, for example when the barometer reading alters by any considerable degree. The average air pressure at sea level is equivalent to 30 inches of mercury. When we are the unwilling recipients of those depressions that seem always to be lurking over Iceland, the pressure may fall to the region of 29 inches and in those memorable periods of a real anticyclone, it may get up to 31 inches. These are large changes of air pressure and they take place quite slowly; our ears are not designed to take notice of them, though other parts of our physiology, particularly our temper, may well do so. If you come down a steep hill fast in a car, however, or if your train runs through a disused subway station at speed, the gradient will sometimes make your ears 'pop'. They are registering the change in air pressure, but the sensation is still not one of sound. In order that you should hear a sound, two other requirements have to be met: first the change must be quite small and second, there must be a change both up and down in a very short time, that is to say there has to be a minute increase of air pressure followed within a fraction of a second by a minute decrease.

Later on we shall look in more detail at the way in which the hearing mechanism works, but over what range of pressures then is the ear sensitive? The smallest change that the ear will take any notice of is equivalent to the atmospheric pressure divided by something over 400,000 billion (4×10^{17}). At the other end of the scale, if the sound pressure changes get too big the ear begins to register, not sound but actual pain (not to be confused with the discomfort which is more psychological than physical of hearing an unpleasant noise like chalk squeaking on a blackboard). In order that the level of actual pain may be reached, the smallest detectable sound pressure has to be multiplied by about one billion.

The second requirement, that there shall be oscillations or alternating changes of pressure, is related to the ear's response to different frequencies. In a young person up to the age of about twenty-five, the ear is capable of detecting as sound a pressure change occurring with a frequency of between 15,000 and 20,000 times a second. This means that one rise and fall of pressure takes no more than one-fifteenth to one-twentieth of a millisecond. As one grows older, one's hearing becomes less able to detect very high frequencies, but most adults can expect to hear frequencies up to about 10,000 cycles per second, that is sounds in which each oscillation takes one-tenth of a millisecond. At the low frequency end of the scale there is not the same decrease in the ear's sensitivity with age, but another factor enters in, whether one is old or young. When we hear any kind of sound which continues for even a short period and appears to have a definite pitch, the ear mechanism is in fact fusing together the successive oscillations into an impression of continuity much in the same way as the eye sees as a moving film something which is in fact a series of still pictures. If the pictures succeed each other too slowly, then the eye no longer gets the impression of movement; similarly with the ear, if the frequency of the oscillations falls below a certain level, then a succession of separate noises is heard instead of a continuous sound. The frequency limit for this effect is in the region of 30 cycles per second and this explains why we may be aware of separate pulses when for instance the lowest note of a large pipe organ is played or when the foghorn of a very large ocean liner is sounded.

We can take the effective range of frequencies occurring in sound-waves for practical purposes as being from 30 to 10,000 cycles per second and the sound-waves of speech fall within this range. It does not very often happen that our ears are exposed to a sound made up of just one frequency of oscillation. When someone is whistling we may hear such a sound and we certainly do if we have occasion to use a tuning-fork for any purpose, but the vast majority of sounds we hear are composed of mixtures of different frequencies sounding at the same time. If we hit middle C on the piano, we hear a musical note which contains within itself a whole range of different frequencies. The lowest of these, if the piano has been properly tuned, will be an oscillation of 261 cycles per second, the fundamental frequency, and all the other frequencies that are sounding with it will be exact multiples of this number; if we multiply 261 by 1, 2, 3, 4, 5 and so on, we get the series of frequencies 522 cycles, 783 cycles, 1044, 1305, 1566, 1827, 2088, 2349, 2610, etc. These are the overtones or harmonics of the fundamental frequency of 261 cycles and a considerable number of them, going up to quite a high frequency, will be present in the sound given out by the single piano string, though they will not all have the same strength.

Suppose that we now strike the next note above, D. This piano string is a little shorter than the middle C string and gives out a note one tone higher with a fundamental frequency of 294 cycles per second. This sound too is a mixture of frequencies, the harmonics of the new note, which are arrived at in the same way as before: they will be 588 cycles, 882, 1176, 1470, 1764, 2058, 2352, 2646, 2940 cycles and so on. This second note is of higher pitch than the first but it is unmistakably a sound produced by a piano. This is because, although the fundamental and harmonic frequencies are different, the relative strength of the various frequencies reproduces very closely the pattern of the middle C. In other words the timbre or quality of the sound given out is determined by the relative strength of the frequencies in the harmonic mixture while the pitch of the note is settled by the actual frequency relations of the fundamental and its harmonics. The violin, the flute, the clarinet and the oboe can all sound middle C and they will all sound different from the piano and from each other. The difference from the piano is partly due to the fact that each of them can continue the sound of the note while the piano tone dies away fairly rapidly after the string has been struck by the hammer, but the real differences in quality stem from the different patterns of harmonics. Notice that the possible frequencies are the same in each case; they are to be found in the first series given for the piano. But in the case of the violin, the lower harmonics will be rather weak while those in the middle to upper range will be rather uniformly strong; the flute tone will have all its strength in the fundamental and the lower harmonics; the clarinet will have most of its strength in the middle harmonics and the oboe will have stronger high harmonics than any of the other instruments, a feature to which it owes its characteristically 'squeaky' tone. When different instruments play the same note, then, what they share is the fundamental frequency and the frequencies in the series of harmonics from which all the notes in the mixture must be taken; when one instrument plays different notes, what the tones have in common is a certain arrangement of the relative strength of the harmonics present in the sound.

When discussing the action of the speech mechanism, we saw that the usual source of sound in speech is the vibration of the vocal cords. The various musical instruments also have to have a source of sound which in all those that have been mentioned is of a different kind. In the piano a hammer strikes a string, in the violin a bow is pulled or pushed across a string, in the flute a stream of breath is directed across a hole in the instrument, in the clarinet a single reed is made to vibrate against a wooden mouthpiece and in the oboe two reeds vibrate against each other. Though the analogy is not exact, there is some resemblance between the larynx mechanism and the double reed of the oboe as a sound source, since the vocal cords, when held together, vibrate against each other in the stream of air coming from the lungs as do the reeds of the oboe in the stream from the player's mouth and lips. The puffs or pulses of air which issue from the vocal cords constitute a sound which is also a mixture made up of a fundamental frequency and a series of harmonics, so that if the larynx is giving out a note at the pitch of middle C, the sound will contain the fundamental of 261 cycles per second and harmonics in the same series as before, 522, 783, 1044, 1305, etc., etc. If the larynx changes its note, there will be a change in the fundamental and in the harmonic series, just as in the case of the musical instruments, so that if it happens to be producing the average frequency for men's voices the fundamental frequency would be 120 cycles per second and the series consequently would be 240, 360, 480, 600, 720, 840 and so on. As in the instruments, the strength of the various harmonics shows a characteristic pattern in the larynx sound: the fundamental is the strongest component of all, the second harmonic is the next strongest, the third the next, and so on, with every harmonic present in the mixture up to quite high frequencies. It may seem surprising that a common pattern should be found in larynx vibrations but this is the fruit of the particular sound-generating mechanism which is in use, just as it is in the case of the oboe; nonetheless one can hear the difference between individual oboes and between oboe players and much more easily of course the difference between individual speakers.

Variation in the frequency of vocal cord vibration, which we saw was necessary as a reflection of the intonation pattern of a spoken message, results in changes in the fundamental frequency of the sound and also in the series of harmonic frequencies that is being produced. We do not ever hear the sound which the larynx generates because the vocal tract is permanently coupled on to the larynx and it modifies in a very drastic way the sound produced at the vocal cords. It is in fact only by inference and by the use of modern scientific instruments that we know what the character of the larynx sound is. In order to explain the effect of the vocal tract upon the larynx sound, something must be said about the phenomenon of resonance.

Most of us are so familiar with the appearance of the common musical instruments that we probably never stop to ask ourselves how they got that way or what the various parts of them are good for. The violinist tucks under his chin a very curiously shaped wooden box equipped with four strings and proceeds to saw away on them with lengths of horsehair, producing sounds which may ravish the soul of the listener with their beauty or may drive him up the wall if the performer is seven years old and a beginner. The real work is being done by setting the four strings into vibration with the bow, so why bother with the box? Wouldn't it do as well to mount the strings on a rectangular wooden block, or a conveniently shaped metal plate, or, since fiddlers' chins get so sore, on a cushion of sponge rubber? We know of course that if we did any of these things, the sound of the violin would not be audible beyond the first row of the stalls. The reason for this is that the body of the violin encloses a volume of air which the vibrating strings force or drive into vibration and the movement of these air particles adds tremendously to the acoustic power put out by the instrument. The air is forced to vibrate because the movement of the strings is communicated to it through the bridge, the sound-post, the bass-bar and the whole body of the fiddle so that all these elements form a resonating system which keeps very much in step with the oscillations of the strings. It would never do therefore to replace this system by one which was incapable of responding in this way.

What considerations determine whether or not the condition of resonance is going to be attained? There are two main ones; they are the material used and the size of the would-be resonator. One can appreciate intuitively that a lump of sponge rubber attached to the strings could do nothing but soak up any acoustic power the latter were putting out and the effect would be quite the reverse of what was desired. Size is important because a resonance effect depends upon the degree of congruence or consonance between the wave-length of the sound being generated and the wave-lengths which the resonator can readily accommodate. To generate low frequency fundamentals we need long strings like those of the double bass and for high ones, the short strings of the violin. It is obvious that double bass players must have a considerable problem in transporting their instruments from place to place; they are stuck with their long strings since nothing else will give the pitch that is needed, but do they have to be attached to such an enormous body and could they not be coupled to something about the size of a biscuit tin? The wave-length of all the notes produced by the double bass is relatively long and so would not fit into a small box or have much effect upon the box itself or the air inside it. Perhaps the thing could be made to work the other way round, for if the body of the violin is so effective a resonator and increases the amount of sound, could one not get even better results by fixing the fourteen-inch strings of the fiddle on to the body of a double bass? Of course the answer is again 'No', because not only are the wave-lengths of the violin notes of the wrong order to evoke resonance in the double bass body but the strength of the vibrations is not enough to impose a great deal of movement upon the large volume of air enclosed there.

The principle of resonance then is that something which is itself vibrating, for example the strings of the instruments, can force into vibration at its own frequency some other system, the resonator, provided the sound generator is efficiently connected up to or coupled with the resonator and provided the resonator is capable of vibrating readily at that frequency, that is to say provided the wave-lengths fit. In speech the main sound source is the larynx and the vocal tract is the resonating system. The relations between the two are extremely complex for a variety of reasons. First, the sound generated by the vocal cord vibration, as we have seen, contains many different frequencies since all the successive harmonics of the fundamental are present up to quite high frequencies. Let us suppose that a man's larynx at a given moment is giving out a tone with a fundamental frequency of 100 cycles per second, to keep the arithmetic as simple as possible. This means that the sound contains the harmonic frequencies 200 cycles, 300, 400, 500, 600 . . . 1500, 1600, 1700, 1800 . . . 2300, 2400, 2500, 2600, 2700 . . . 3300, 3400, 3500 and so on up to 4000 cycles or more. The resonating system, the vocal tract, will respond to any frequency or frequencies in this series whose wave-lengths happen to fit in with its own dimensions. The result is that, in the sound which finally comes out of the speaker's mouth, any of the harmonics which hit off the resonances of the tract will be relatively strong and those which do not will be very weak.

In the larynx sound, as we noted earlier, the fundamental is the strongest component and the harmonics gradually decrease in strength as we go upwards in frequency. The average length of a man's vocal tract is 17 centimetres and the full wave-length of most of the fundamental frequencies generated by the male larynx is many times greater than this. A fundamental of 100 cycles per second has a wave-length which is twenty times the length of the vocal tract and even the quarter wave-length, which can provide a basis for resonance, is still five times as long. One invariable effect of the vocal tract therefore is to reduce the strength of the fundamental frequency of the larynx tone compared with that of higher harmonics.

A resonating system will generally have more than one area of resonance on the frequency scale. The body of the violin would not be very satisfactory if it responded only to notes on the D string, let us say. The vocal tract with the column of air which it encloses also has a number of resonances. From the point of view of speech as an expression of language, three main resonances in the tract are important, though others may well be evoked by the voice quality of individual speakers. The second factor which makes relations between the larynx and the vocal tract so complicated is linked with the operation of these resonances. A unique feature of the speech mechanism as a sound-producing instrument is that the resonances are not fixed but can be shifted about along the frequency scale. Our articulatory view of speech showed that differences between sounds were brought about by continual movement of the tongue, soft palate, lips and so on. The acoustic effect of these movements is to vary the internal dimensions of the vocal tract so that its resonances change, thus bringing about changes in the relative strength of the harmonics and hence in the quality of the sound which issues from the speaker's mouth. Movements of the tongue have a major effect on the resonances of the vocal tract so it will be useful to see in principle the sort of thing that happens. If you say aloud the word *he* and keep it going on one note for a bit, you will notice that your tongue is bunched up rather towards the front of the mouth; the vowel itself sounds thin and, if exaggerated, almost squeaky. Now change to saying *ha* in the same way, and the tongue is lying much flatter on the floor of the mouth, the sound is rounder and has no particular edge on it. For the vowel of *he*, the lowest resonance of the vocal tract is quite low down in the frequency scale; if you happened to be using a fundamental of 100 cycles per second it was probably at 300 cycles; the second resonance however is high up, probably at 2100 cycles. When you change to *ha*, because of the move of the tongue both these resonances shift, the lower one to a higher frequency, probably at 700 cycles, and the second resonance comes a long way down to 900 cycles. The third resonance in both cases is probably at the same frequency, most likely 2400 or 2500 cycles. The high second resonance gives the first vowel its slightly squeaky quality and the nearness of the two resonances, the greater roundness to the second vowel. A series of words such as *heed, hid, head, had, hard* gives rise to a progression of tongue movements and hence a progressive coming together of the first and second resonances from the arrangement for *he* to that for *ha*.

This brings us to one of the most important, indeed an indispensable, feature of the speech mechanism as an acoustic system. In the examples above we have related the resonance frequencies to a fundamental of 100 cycles per second, but in speech the fundamental frequency of the larynx tone is varying all the time, so what happens to the resonances when this occurs? Let us see what the situation will be if we change the fundamental frequency from 100 to 120 cycles per second. There will no longer be harmonics at the frequencies 300 and 2100 cycles, which were the resonances for *he*, nor at 700 and 900 cycles for *ha*; but there will be harmonics at 360 and at 2160 cycles, and also at 720 and 960 cycles. The acoustic properties of the vocal tract are such that each resonance is spread over a certain range of frequencies; in other words it is not sharply tuned to specific resonance frequencies but can be forced into vibration by any frequencies that are reasonably near to the optimum condition for resonance. Because the larynx tone contains the successive harmonics of each fundamental, it does not matter how this fundamental changes, there is always some harmonic that is near enough to evoke the neighbouring resonance of the vocal tract. The location of the various resonances in the frequency range is settled by the shape of the vocal tract, which is in turn characteristic of a given vowel, so that when the same shape recurs, there are going to be prominent harmonics at roughly the same places in the frequency scale even though the fundamental frequency is varying all the time.

This feature of the speech mechanism is a vital one, for without it the language system simply would not work. If things

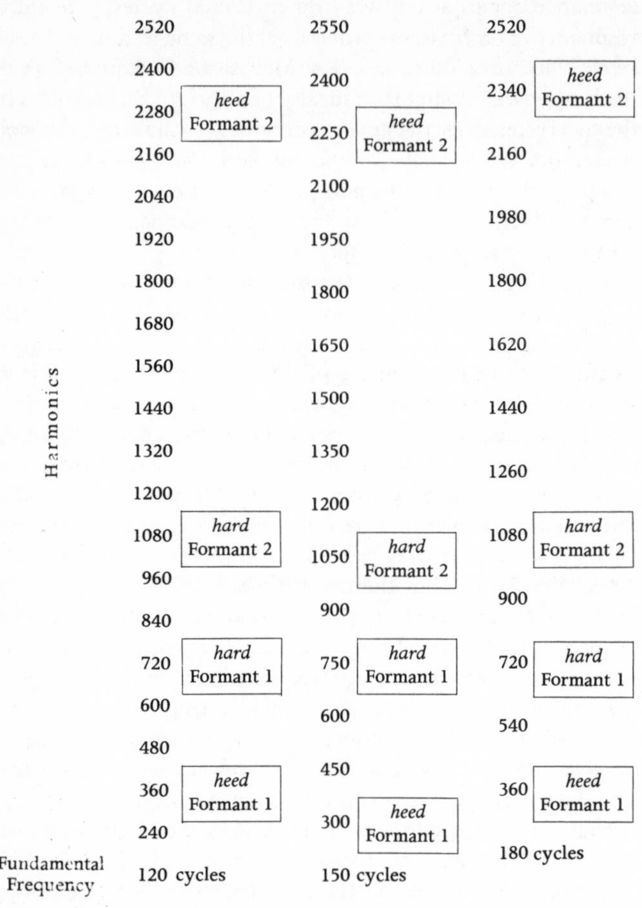

The larynx produces different fundamental frequencies as the pitch of the voice changes and each fundamental frequency generates a different series of harmonics, as in the three examples shown above. The higher the fundamental, the wider the spacing between successive harmonics. No matter how the fundamental frequency changes in speech, there are always harmonics close to the resonances of the vocal tract for different vowels and these provide the formants, as is shown for the vowels of *heed* and *hard* in this table.

were otherwise, we should hear a marked change in sound quality as the pitch of the voice altered; the vowel of the word *heed* would have quite different colours when said on a high pitch and a low one, to say nothing of how different it would sound when uttered by a man, woman and child. As it is, we have no difficulty in recognizing the 'same' sound in the speech of one person on many different occasions and in the speech of many different people; this is why it is possible to transpose the language form of a message into sound-waves and for the listener to recover the language form.

Because the resonances of the vocal tract perform this important function and because a particular arrangement of resonances is characteristic of a given sound, a special term is used in this context to refer to the resonance frequencies: they are called *formants* and they are labelled by numbering them from the lowest resonance upwards. The first resonance of the tract is Formant 1, the second Formant 2, the next Formant 3 and if there are higher ones they are numbered successively. Most of the distinctions on which the language system depends are carried by Formants 1 and 2, though Formant 3 has certain functions which we shall come to later on. In the first example above, the vowel of *he* had Formant 1 at 300 cycles and Formant 2 at 2100 cycles when the fundamental was 100 cycles, and there was a shift of Formant 1 to 360 and of Formant 2 to 2160 cycles when the fundamental rose to 120 cycles. The series *heed, hid, head, had, hard* contains vowels in which Formants 1 and 2 come progressively closer together.

Vowel phonemes which are represented by diphthongs involve a movement of the tongue from one vowel articulation to another in the course of one syllable. Such a movement must change the resonances of the vocal tract and so shift the formants. In a word like *hide,* for example, the formants are first close together, the configuration characteristic of *ha,* but they then separate and move towards the locations found in *hid*. It is this movement of Formants I and 2 that leads us to recognize *hide* as being different from *hard* (in the speech of southern England!).

So far we have talked about resonances and formants only

in connection with vowels, but it is clear that every movement that affects the vocal tract, no matter what kind of sound is being produced, must have a similar effect. A number of the sounds which correspond to consonant phonemes are acoustically very much like vowels and among these is the very interesting group of the nasal sounds, /m, n, ng/. In articulating these sounds the soft palate is lowered so that the side branch of the vocal tract leading through the nose is connected with the main air column. The acoustic effect of this is to add, not a resonance but an anti-resonance, that is to say that the strength of a particular range of harmonics is reduced in comparison with the condition in which the nasal branch is shut off. The anti-resonance affects mainly the frequency range where the second formant of vowel sounds tends to be located, that is from about 900 to 2000 cycles per second. Each of the nasal sounds therefore tends to have a particularly low first formant and then there is little acoustic energy until we reach the level where the third formant of vowels appears, that is from about 2000 to 2500 cycles; naturally this constitutes the second formant for the nasal consonant.

The sounds for /l/ and /r/ resemble the vowels more closely than do the nasal consonants since they are made with the passage to the nose shut off and do not show the anti-resonance effect. Formants 1 and 2 have a very similar configuration for both sounds and the distinction between them is carried mainly by Formant 3 which shows a considerable movement in frequency for /r/ but remains comparatively steady in the course of /l/.

There are, however, a good many sounds in speech which, as we saw in the previous chapter, depend on the generation of noise somewhere in the vocal tract. Do the vocal tract resonances have any influence on these sounds and, if so, how does this come about? The short answer is that the noises are indeed affected by vocal tract resonances and that this must be so since those resonances are a property of the tract itself and not of any sound source that may be in action. We must first, however, see what is implied in the action of a noise generator and how it differs from the tone generator in the larynx.

Speech noises are produced, as was said earlier, by forcing a certain amount of air to flow rapidly through a rather narrow gap. The result is a random movement of the air particles very different from that set up by the rhythmic opening and closing of the vocal cords. It is the periodic nature of the latter which leads to the generation of a fundamental frequency and its associated series of harmonics. The turbulent movement of air particles set up in the noise generator produces a random mixture of frequencies which are not related to each other in any way, instead of the neat arrangement of numbers obtained by multiplying a given fundamental frequency by successive whole numbers. Usually such turbulence creates a sound with a very wide range of frequencies in the mixture. An example from everyday life which illustrates something of its character is the sound of fat frying in a pan. When we hear this sound we have the impression that it is a rather high-pitched hissing, but if other sounds are going on at the same time, we find that the noise obliterates all sounds about equally; it will drown the sound of music from a radio and will also drown conversation, masking both the low and the high frequency sounds of speech. Such a noise is called a *white noise*, because it has all frequencies in it, on the analogy of white light which contains light of all wave-lengths.

The noises generated in speech are basically of this character; the fact that they do not all sound like fat frying is due to the modification of the noise by vocal tract resonances. These resonances will work just as well on noise as on periodic sounds and there is a simple way of demonstrating this fact. When we whisper, the vibration of the vocal cords is switched off and no periodic sound is generated at the larynx; the tone is replaced by noise generated by forcing air rapidly through a gap between the vocal cords without setting them into vibration and this noise travels upwards through the vocal tract. A whispered remark is just as intelligible to anyone near enough to hear it as one said in an ordinary voice. This is because all the usual variations in the resonances of the tract are taking place and are shaping the noise just as ordinarily they shape the voiced sound. It happens that in whisper the noise is being generated at one end of the vocal tract, in the larynx, but wherever the noise is set up, it will be fed into the whole tract and will be shaped by its resonances.

This being the case we should expect that speech noises, by the time they leave the lips of the speaker, would be characterized by formants in the same way as vowels are and to some extent this is true. However, in dealing with consonant sounds and in particular the noises, it is usual to refer to the vocal tract as having a filtering effect on the noise. An acoustic filter performs a function analogous to that of any other type of filter: it keeps out certain things, just as the filter tip of a cigarette is supposed to keep out the noxious tobacco tars. The speech mechanism generates basically a white noise and the effect of the vocal tract is to filter out, that is to reduce in strength, the frequencies over certain parts of the wide range which the word 'white' implies. The specific filtering effect associated with any articulation will depend very much on where the noise generator is sited in the vocal tract because this determines the length of the branches of the tract on either side of the generator. Very broadly speaking, the farther forward in the tract the noise generator is situated, the more the lower part of the noise will be filtered out, though the acoustic effects are infinitely more complex than this would suggest. In English, for example, the sound for /s/ is generated at the gums of the upper teeth; in this case the noise is filtered in such a way that practically all the noise components below a frequency of about 4000 cycles per second are suppressed and we therefore hear a quite high-pitched hissing in this sound. The sound for /sh/ is made a little farther back in the vocal tract and also, incidentally, with a rather wider gap for the air to rush through; the filter in this case allows lower frequency components to pass, down to about 2000 cycles, and the hissing sounds correspondingly lower in pitch. If you make the two sounds one after the other, you can hear this difference in pitch quite clearly, rather as if one were whistling two notes, although both are noises. The sounds for /th/ and /f/ arise from turbulence set up farther forward than for /s/; both sounds contain noise components spread over rather a wide range and both are comparatively weak sounds. The filtering effect in both of them is such that the main acoustic energy lies in the top part of the frequency range, between 6000 and 8000 cycles. From the point of view of the actual noise there is very little to distinguish the two sounds from each other and they are in fact quite difficult to differentiate out of context. We shall see in the next chapter what other means are found to make the distinction.

The short explosive noises that accompany the articulations for /p/, /t/ and /k/ are equally subject to the filtering effect of the vocal tract. If you say the three words *par*, *tar* and *car* fairly forcefully you will be able to detect the difference in the noise that precedes the vowel in each case. The articulation for /p/ takes place at the extreme front end of the vocal tract and when the lips are separated, the resonance of the whole tract behind the closure tends to throw into prominence the lower frequency components in the noise. In /t/, on the other hand, the explosion at the level of the teeth ridge emphasizes mainly high frequency components and we hear a high-pitched burst of noise. The closure of the tract for /k/ takes place at the soft palate approximately at the mid-point of the length of the tract, and the noise for this sound is at a middle frequency between those for /p/ and /t/.

We have now looked at examples of the classes of sound that speech gives rise to, without of course attempting an exhaustive account of all those that occur in one language system. In the course of a single remark the articulatory mechanism is on the move practically the whole of the time. Whenever the sounds are voiced, the vocal cords are vibrating and generating a periodic sound or tone of which the fundamental frequency and hence the string of harmonics are varying continuously. This periodic sound excites the resonances of the vocal tract and these in turn impose upon it the formants which shape the sound that comes from the speaker's mouth and nose. The fact that the mechanism is continually moving means that the formant frequencies are changing almost all the time. Certain sounds in the course of the utterance require that a noise generator shall be brought into action and this is situated at any one of a number of points along the vocal tract. The resulting noise is filtered by the resonances of the tract so that noise energy is concentrated in different parts of the frequency range. Sometimes the noise is accompanied by larynx tone and when this happens, there is a low frequency sound coming from the larynx as well as the characteristic noise for the given consonant.

One further aspect of the speech sound-waves remains to be mentioned. So far we have been mainly concerned with the various frequencies that make up these sound-waves. When discussing the syllable, we saw that there are continual fluctuations in the volume of the sound that comes from the speaker and this is a factor which has considerable importance from the language point of view. The physical measurement involved here is that of sound pressure, which has already been referred to, or of the power, energy or intensity of the sound. Our everyday experience makes us familiar with the measurement of power in terms of watts. We know that a 100 watt light bulb gives out more light and consumes more power than a 60 watt bulb. Acoustic power can be measured in the same units and if we turn up the volume control of a radio set, the loudspeaker gives out more watts of sound energy. In the context of speech and of acoustics generally the levels of power that have to be considered are infinitesimally small compared with those familiar to us through the operation of electricity. The faintest sound our ears can hear, which was mentioned earlier in terms of sound pressure, is a sound whose power is 10^{-16} watts. If this expression happens to mean little or nothing to you, you can get an idea of what it signifies by writing down a decimal point followed by fifteen noughts and then the figure 1 with the word watt after it. The power level of ordinary speech is many times greater than this but even so it is at a very low level. It has been estimated that it takes a million people all talking at the same time to put out power equivalent to that of a 60 watt light bulb. Evidently the power of the spoken word does not lie in the physical domain and is not going to solve any power crises by direct application.

One of the problems posed by the measurement of acoustic

power or intensity is that of finding a suitable unit or scale with which to express the measurements. This is due not so much to the very small amounts of power with which one is dealing, since one can coin a name for a very small unit, but to the fact that sounds differ so widely in intensity that comparing them involves numbers that are almost astronomical. If you are listening to someone who is talking to you in a normal conversational tone, the general level of acoustic power that is reaching your ear is already one million times greater than that of the faintest sound that can be heard. The solution that is commonly adopted is to use the decibel as the unit of measurement. The word is familiar enough to us nowadays; it occasionally makes the headlines in newspapers or magazines where it tends to appear as the 'deadly decibel', though in other contexts the 'dulcet decibel' would be just as applicable. As a unit of measurement the decibel is a somewhat curious animal and it is necessary to say a word or two about its peculiarities.

The unit originally used was the *bel*, equal to ten decibels, and this was named by telephone engineers to commemorate Alexander Graham Bell, the inventor of the telephone. He was an engineering student in Edinburgh and in London in the 1860s and his father, Alexander Melville Bell, was a well-known authority on speech. Alexander Graham Bell went later to America where, in the course of inventing a hearing aid for his deaf wife, he invented the telephone. Those to whom the telephone has become much more a bane than a blessing may be inclined to view this as doing a great wrong to do a little right. In the United States the telephone service almost everywhere is run by the Bell System, and this great organization stems from the pioneer work of Alexander Graham Bell. The bel proved in practice to be rather too large and has been replaced by a unit one-tenth the size, the decibel.

The first feature of the decibel is that it denotes a relative measure and not an absolute one, in other words it expresses the ratio between two sound intensities. In view of its origin this is not surprising; if someone is talking at one end of a telephone line from London to Glasgow, a matter of most practical interest is how much the power of the speech has decreased by the time it arrives in Glasgow. Such a quantity is most conveniently measured in decibels, since when a figure in decibels is given, it means that the intensity of some particular sound is so many times greater than that of another sound. This might seem to be contradicted by the fact that newspaper reports and other sources most frequently assign a number of decibels to just one sound. We are told that the level of noise from a pneumatic drill reached 90 db. or that the noise from Concorde on landing and take-off is no more than 120 db. Such figures contain a hidden comparison with the value 10^{-16} watts, already mentioned as the level of the faintest sound the ear can detect, so the statements really mean that the noise of the drill was 90 db. more intense, the aircraft noise 120 db. more intense than a sound with this threshold value. Since the numbers quoted have a common reference level, we can justifiably compare the two and deduce that the aircraft noise is 30 db. more intense than that of the pneumatic drill.

This comparison serves to illustrate a second advantage of the decibel as a unit of measurement, the fact that it brings the whole scale of power ratios to manageable proportions. The sound of the pneumatic drill is actually one thousand million times as intense as the threshold sound and the Concorde noise is one thousand times more intense again. On the decibel scale these enormous ratios are expressed in at the most three digit numbers. This is due to the fact that the decibel is a logarithmic unit, that is to say all numbers are given as a power of 10. We write down the fact that one hundred is ten squared by putting 10^2, that one thousand is ten cubed by putting 10^3 and so on. These indices give the logarithm of the number and as, in working with decibels, it is understood that everything is referred to the base 10, we can write down the index by itself. All we need to remember is that the logarithm of the intensity ratio gives the answer in bels and each bel equals 10 decibels. If one sound then is 100 times as intense as another, the ratio is one hundred to one and the logarithm, as we have just seen, is 2. The difference between the two sounds is therefore 2 bels or 20 decibels. In a case where a sound is one thousand times as intense as another, as in our comparison of the pneumatic drill and Concorde, the difference amounts to 3 bels or 30 db. Naturally calculations are not limited to cases where the ratio is conveniently a multiple of ten, for any number can be expressed as a logarithm to the base ten. The logarithm of the number 2 is equal to 0·3, so if one sound is double the intensity of another, the difference is 0·3 of a bel or 3 db.

This explanation will perhaps help to make somewhat more meaningful a discussion of speech intensities in terms of decibels. The fluctuations in volume or intensity due to the nature of the syllables in any utterance are themselves variations around some general level which depends on just how loudly or softly the speaker is talking. This again depends partly on how much noise there is going on, but in ordinary conversation carried on in a quiet room the average intensity is likely to be about 60 db. Notice that this figure is given without any explicit comparison, so it must refer to the standard threshold level. It implies that the ratio between conversational speech and the reference level has a logarithm of 6 and is therefore one million. Obviously the intensity of a sound falls away as one gets farther from the source, so we need to qualify our statement by saying that 60 db. is just about the intensity of sound that would reach the ear of a listener who is three feet away from the speaker. How much more power could we put out in speech than we usually do in conversation? This certainly varies with individuals but if you were to shout as loudly as you can, it is unlikely that you would be able to raise the average intensity of your speech by more than about 15 db., bringing it up to 75 db. At the other end of the scale, if you drop your voice to an extremely confidential tone without actually whispering, the level might fall to about 40 db.

To obtain such average figures it is necessary to make continuous measurements over some period and to take the mean intensity values. During this time the string of syllables will be the factor mainly responsible for the variations. If we take the conversational level of 60 db. as the basis, the greatest contribution to the general intensity level will be made by the vowel parts of the syllables; these occupy the major part of the time and will all be near to or above 60 db. Many of the consonant sounds on the other hand will fall well below this intensity. We can in fact scale out all the sounds in the English system according to the average intensity relations between them. To do this we might take the sound with the lowest intensity, which is /th/ in *thin*, and find out how many decibels difference there was between this and all the other sounds. The greatest difference will be in the vowels, and among them those with the most open vocal tract will give the highest values; these are the vowels of *thought* and *hard* which on average are about 26 db. above the level of /th/. In the one syllable *thought*, therefore, there is a fluctuation in acoustic power of this amount. Vowels with a narrower tract, like the one in *thin*, are about 23 db. above /th/. The consonants in general come lower down the scale, with such sounds as /f/, /p/ and /k/ some 7 to 10 db. more intense than /th/. The sound /sh/ is a fairly intense noise since, as we have seen, the noise components spread over quite a wide range of frequencies and it comes close to the vowels at about 18 db., while /s/ is somewhat lower at 12 db. In the course of any spoken message, then, such variations of up to about 26 db. are taking place in the overall power that is being put out; when the average intensity of the speech changes, that is we speak more loudly or more quietly, the intensity relations between the sounds are not in fact so very much affected.

By means of all these very complex variations in both frequency and intensity, the sound-waves of speech reflect all the distinctions that the language form of the message demands. The articulatory form of speech is already complicated enough, yet the acoustic form is even more so. At least it can be said that, thanks to modern methods of research, we understand a good deal about the processes by which the articulatory mechanism generates the sound-waves of speech. The latter provide the input to the ear and brain of the listener, which have the job of getting back to the language form of the spoken message and we shall see in the next chapter that this is very far from being a straightforward task.

5

Speech as ear-work

Where more is meant than meets the ear. — Milton

The brain plays as major a role in the reception of speech as in its production, and much of this chapter will be concerned with the way in which the brain deals with the sounds that come into our ears when someone is talking. It will be useful to say something first, however, about the working of the hearing mechanism as a piece of receiving apparatus.

The sound-waves generated by the speech mechanism travel outwards from the speaker in all directions and some of their energy arrives at the ear of the listener. The minute changes in air pressure cause very small movements in the various mechanical parts that make up the ear and we have already seen that the changes must be oscillations, that is changes in two directions, if we are to have any sensation of sound. The resulting movements in the ear are to and fro movements. The ears themselves, that is the part that is stuck on the outside of the head, no longer have a very important function in our present stage of evolution since we have lost the capacity for pricking up our ears. The external ear does do something, however, as we know when we get to the age for cupping the hand round the ear in order to increase its efficiency in locating a source of sound. Inside the ear is the ear-drum, a membrane which is made to move in and out by the arrival of sound-waves. A small increase in pressure makes the drum move inwards and the next drop in pressure draws it outward again. On the inner side of the drum is a chain of very small bones which transmits the movement to a tiny membrane set in the innermost part of the ear. The inner ear contains the nerve endings whose job it is to forward auditory information to the brain; they are set in a special fluid and respond to waves generated in this fluid by the movements of the drum, the bones and the inner membrane. By means of this mechanism sound-waves reaching the external ear are converted into nerve impulses which pass on the information they carry to the brain.

An important point about the movements of the hearing mechanism is that they are mechanical, that is to say we do not have voluntary control over them. We can control the action of our eyes to a certain extent because we can decide to close them. We have no means of doing the same with our ears; when sound-waves arrive, our ear-drums have to flap, and we all know from experience that they are not off duty even when we are asleep. This state of affairs is in sharp contrast to the conditions in the speech production mechanism where the movements are voluntary and therefore require an enormous amount of practice in the learning stage. There is no kind of practice in speech reception that we can do with our ears alone; all the learning goes on in the brain.

From one point of view the sounds of speech are just like any other sounds. The information sent on from the ear to the brain in the form of nerve impulses causes us to perceive all sounds in a variety of ways. We perceive some as being high-pitched, others as being lower, some as loud, others soft, some last a long time while others are shorter and, most important of all for speech, we perceive that sounds differ in their quality or colour. There is no standard set of adjectives to express the last kind of variation; we appreciate a basic difference between noises and tones and apart from this we may judge the quality to be shrill, mellow, harsh, piercing, round, grating, smooth or any one of a dozen other things. The sounds of speech make the same kind of perceptual impression on us but we do not characterize them in the same way. The brain has very complex and quite specific methods of organizing the acoustic information from speech and it does not apply these to any other kind of input from the ears. It is therefore the brain's organization of incoming acoustic information that we must look at in order to understand something about the reception of speech, and it is this that constitutes the real ear-work of speech.

The point has already been made that speech can be understood only if speaker and listener have a common language and it is obvious that a listener, when he takes in speech, must make great use of those stores of language information which he carries in his brain. Listening to speech, like talking, is something we learn to do in our very early years and in fact the ability to receive speech is always in advance of the ability to produce it. Both are learned so thoroughly that we pay them no attention so it is not easy to appreciate that the converting of speech sound-waves back into language units is one part of the whole process which it is the hardest to give a satisfactory account of.

We know what someone has said to us because we have heard the same sounds before, we have heard the same words before and if we have not heard the same sentences, we have heard something very like them. The problem seems to be very simple, then; we are recognizing things because they are the same as things we have experienced before. But if we look very closely at the situation we see that this is not an accurate statement and that it glosses over difficulties that are implicit in every kind of recognition, whether of something we hear or see or even smell, taste or touch. The parallel with things seen is probably the most useful one. Day after day we see the same scenes, the same people, the same objects and if there should be an exception, we remark on the fact by saying 'I've never seen that before'. We recognize our family, our friends, our house, the streets and the buildings because we have seen the same sights before. Or have we? If we consider what is actually coming into our eyes, it is a physical fact that we never see the same sight twice. With every passing moment changes take place, in the light for one thing, and in the people, the objects and the scenes we are looking at. Even if we gaze at the 'same' scene at 10 a.m. on successive days, in a period of absolutely settled weather, the light has changed and will never be the same again. Of course we quite rightly pay no attention to all this, but it serves to show that we have a rather special notion of what it means to see the same thing. It means among other things that we have learned very efficiently to disregard a great many differences which are perfectly visible to us and to notice a limited number of features which persist in some degree through the many changing versions of things and people that are presented to our eyes. It is this process we call recognition, and life would be well-nigh impossible without it. Once a person has become familiar to us we can recognize him by his height, his build, his gait, his clothes, his hair and so on, even at a distance or in a poor light, and we may say 'I would know so-and-so anywhere by his walk'. What we have developed is a pattern of visible features, almost a formula, by which we recognize our friend or relation despite the many real changes in appearance that he or she undergoes. We are quick to notice when the pattern itself is disturbed and it is this which leads us to make such remarks as 'Why, you've shaved off your moustache' or 'You've had your hair done!'.

If it is true that our eyes never see the same thing twice, the case is the same but to a far greater degree with the sounds we hear in speech. When we recognize a house at least the same bricks and mortar stand in front of us, but taking in speech requires that we should recognize as the 'same' sounds that differ from each other in a dozen different ways and can never in the nature of things be identical. We listen to a hundred different speakers and in the course of what they say we recognize the same word over and over again, yet the sounds they produce even for the same word vary tremendously. Some of the speakers are men, some women, some children; their larynxes differ in size and give out different ranges of frequency; their vocal tracts too have different dimensions and impose different formants at different places in the frequency scale. The various individuals have been brought up in different parts of the country and may have widely different pronunciations for the same word, they may even operate slightly different phonemic systems. Every individual speaker has his own voice quality, so much so that, with people we know well, we recognize the voice and we can in any case tell two voices apart when they are saying the same words. One single speaker will sound different on different occasions; the sounds he is giving out will be changed by his having a cold, and changed again depending on whether it is a cold in the head, the throat or the chest. These are just some of the types of variation in sound that we take in our stride when we recognize the same words. Then, to narrow the time scale of the variations, in the course of one remark by a speaker the larynx frequency is varying continuously, as we have seen, with a consequent change in the series of harmonic frequencies being generated from moment to moment. We find no difficulty in recognizing a word when it is said with a rising tone in a question and with a falling tone in a statement or with any appropriate intonation and rhythm pattern.

Finally there is a source of variation in speech sounds which has so far scarcely been mentioned and that is the effect of one sound in the string upon neighbouring sounds. The articulatory movements made in one utterance are all joined together, in fact the utterance is one continuous movement. We do not set the speech mechanism in a suitable posture for making, say, a /k/ and then leap smartly to another position to make a vowel; there is a smooth transition between the movements and hence the sounds which come out are affected by the direction in which movements have been made, that is by the sounds that precede and follow. You can hear such an effect, for instance, if you say aloud the two words *keep cool* and as you are saying them listen very carefully to the first sound in each word; the burst of noise for /k/ is of a distinctly higher pitch in *keep* than it is in *cool*, a difference which will probably be more obvious if you whisper the words. This means that the following vowel is having an influence on the consonant sound, the vowel made farther forward in the vocal tract, *keep*, leading to a higher frequency noise than the one made farther back, *cool*. This kind of interaction between the sounds that occur in one string is common to all languages and affects many of the features that characterize sound qualities. In the course of the articulatory description of 'I don't think I can', we noted that because of the presence of /th/ at the beginning of *think*, both the preceding /t/ and the /n/ are made with the tongue against the top teeth instead of against the gums. This shift of articulation alters the quality of these two sounds but as English listeners we do not detect the change because it does not affect the meaning of the remark. This illustrates a general law about the sound variations brought about by context and that is that modifications can be made so as to reduce the amount of movement on the part of the speech mechanism provided they do not lead to a confusion between one phoneme and another which would change the meaning. The English system does not use two nasal sounds for distinguishing words, one made at the teeth and the other at the gums, so the modification in question can be made. Suppose the effect had worked in the reverse direction and that, because both /n/ and /t/ are made at the gums, the first noise in *think* were made in the same place, this would produce the sound for /s/ and hence the word *sink*. Such a change is never regularly made by English speakers, though one may certainly hear the substitution in the speech of non-native speakers of English; in that case, for reasons which we shall be looking at in the next chapter, we still manage to understand what has been said.

These effects of sounds in context are yet another source of variation to be added to all those mentioned above. Although the variability of speech sounds is decidedly less in one speaker than in a hundred different people, we are still not hearing the same sounds when listening to one person. What is in fact happening is that we carry a set of categories of sound in our brain, and here we see the basic importance of the language system, and we also carry the criteria according to which we sort everything that comes in during speech into one of these categories. In order to do this, very far from recognizing the same sound, we have to disregard many differences in sound quality that are really there and pay attention to a few particular features which tell us which box to sort the sound into. This is the same kind of job we do when we say 'With that hair and those glasses, it must be Joe'. We have learned to use certain items of acoustic information in this way, certain features of the sounds. The name given to these features is acoustic 'cues' because their presence cues the recognition of a particular phoneme, intonation or rhythmic pattern. We have already encountered examples of these cues in the acoustic description of speech sounds: the formants of vowel sounds are important because they act as cues for different vowel phonemes; the way in which noise is filtered by the vocal tract provides cues for the recognition of consonants and the switching on and off of the vocal cord vibrations affords another kind of cue.

It is not immediately obvious in what sense such features act as cues since they appear to be simply aspects of the acoustic version of speech which the ear will take in anyway. There are three things about acoustic cues which make them play a vital role in speech reception. First they are qualities of the sound which we notice at the expense of some other qualities; they occupy as it were the foreground of our auditory attention, allowing some other features to sink into the background or in certain circumstances to be used for quite other purposes. A good example of this is the matter of voice quality. When we recognize a vowel spoken by someone as representing a given phoneme, we are discounting all the elements peculiar to the individual voice of the speaker, yet this information is available to a different part of our attention when we recognize a person's voice. So we might think of the cue method as a means of heightening contrast, as it were, of making certain things stand out against the acoustic background.

The other two facts about acoustic cues are, second, that their basic function is to enable the language system to work and, third, that they always refer to relative differences between sounds and not to any absolute qualities. These two properties are so bound up together that they have to be considered in conjunction. To take a straightforward example, the first two vowel formants, that is the two lowest resonances of the vocal tract (see p. 5), act as cues which can be used in identifying any of the words *heed, hid, head, had, hard.* The function of the cue is simply to keep these words distinct from each other (and of course many others, since we are dealing with only a small part of the English vowel system). The actual frequencies of Formants 1 and 2 will certainly vary from speaker to speaker, so the cue is found in the *relation* of these formants: they must be spaced farther apart in *heed* than they are in *hid*, they must be closer together in *hard* than they are in *had*, and so on. As long as these relations are maintained, the different vowels are easily identifiable and when we have heard a few words from a complete stranger, we are able to set up a framework with reference to which we have no difficulty in recognizing his various vowel sounds. We can predict from past experience how the relations are likely to be set out. The formant frequencies generated in the vocal tract of a small child are different in some appreciable degree from those in a man, that is if we take average values, but we take this into account when we hear a child talking and we base our recognition on his system of formants, which preserves the relations but with different actual formant frequencies.

There have been some intriguing demonstrations of this using synthesized speech, that is speech produced by electronic circuits and untouched by human tongue or lips. With such devices it is possible to shift formant frequencies about at will and to combine them with different fundamental frequencies. Let us imagine that we manufacture a word with the formant frequencies one would find in a child's pronunciation of the word *head* and we plant this in a sentence where the formants of all the other vowels are also appropriate to a child's speech. In these conditions everyone who hears it is satisfied that the word is *head*. But if we now take exactly the same syllable and insert it in a sentence where the formants of all the other vowels are those suitable to a man's vocal tract, everyone who hears it in these conditions recognizes the word as *hid* and not *head*, because this is where the formant configuration of the syllable fits into the new framework. This is a very convincing demonstration that acoustic cues in speech are by nature concerned with relations between sounds; their job is to make the language system work and all language systems are based on the relations between the elements within the system.

Among such elements are the phonemes and we have already seen that language systems may differ from each other at the phoneme level. Acoustic cues are a means of making sure that all the sounds the listener receives go into the right phoneme boxes. In a language like English where /s/ and /sh/ are different phonemes, there have to be suitable cues for distinguishing them; in Dutch and Spanish, as we saw, there are not two separate boxes for such sounds and therefore speakers of these languages do not have a cue with which to separate them. The phoneme system has to work as a whole, that is to say that every phoneme has to be kept distinct from every other and consequently the acoustic cues work systematically. The principle can be illustrated by looking at one small part of the English phoneme system. English listeners can identify any one of the four words *fie, thigh, sigh* and *shy* by means of the first sound that is heard in them. They are all noises filtered in different ways and lasting about the same length of time, and all voiceless, that is without any accompanying vibration of the vocal cords. There is one cue which we use to split the four sounds into two pairs: the first two noises are comparatively weak and the second two are quite strong, the average difference between the pairs being about 10 db. If in this context a weak noise is heard, it must be the beginning of *fie* or *thigh*; if a strong one, it must be *sigh* or *shy*. The second pair can be sorted from each other according to the character or pitch of the noise, as we saw earlier, so that if the strong noise is high-pitched, it is identified as /s/ and if it is low-pitched, as /sh/. The two weaker noises, however, both have the greatest acoustical energy in the high frequency range and are very difficult to distinguish on the basis of the noise alone. For this purpose we use another kind of cue and one that is employed in many different contexts. Whenever there is a rapid movement somewhere in the vocal tract there is an equally rapid change in the vocal tract resonances which produce a switch in formant frequency, referred to as a formant transition. In a majority of cases a consonant movement comes immediately before or immediately after a vowel articulation so that nearly all vowel formants show transitions. The formant transition is one of the most frequently used cues in speech and it serves a variety of purposes in distinguishing one sound from another. A Formant 2 transition, for example, is particularly important in sorting sounds made at different places in the vocal tract and in the case we have just been considering, it is this cue mainly that helps us to distinguish between /f/ and /th/. In the first of these the noise is made at the lower lip and in the second, behind the upper teeth; the move from these articulations to the following vowel imposes different transitions on the second formant, we hear the difference and use it as a cue in identifying the two sounds.

When speech is coming in, the brain is able to assign the sounds to the right phonemes by combining together cues which it has learned to employ for the purpose; for the initial sounds of *fie, thigh, sigh* and *shy* it uses the difference in strength, in pitch and in second formant transition. The general usefulness of the formant transition cue can be exemplified by the group of sounds /p, t, k/. When sounds representing these phonemes occur right at the end of a remark, very frequently there is no burst of noise so that the last syllable ends with the silence caused by closing off the vocal tract completely. If any of the words *map, mat* or *mack* were in this position, we should still have no difficulty in knowing which had occurred because the transition at the end of the vowel would be different in each case. It is this effect in the word *cocktail,* given earlier as an example, that tells us there is a /k/ in the middle of the word although there is no burst of noise to represent it.

Much the same kind of thing happens in the case of the nasal consonants /m, n, ng/. The formants for these sounds given earlier, one very low formant and another just above the frequency of most vowel second formants, are a cue for the whole group of nasal consonants; it simply tells us that a nasal consonant has occurred but on this cue alone we cannot tell which of the three it is. The closing of the lips for /m/, the contact of the tongue with the upper gums for /n/ and of the back of the tongue with the soft palate for /ng/ each causes a different glide in formant frequency which enables us to tell the difference, for example, between *ram, ran* and *rang*.

In cases where the articulatory movement takes place rather more slowly, formant transitions are also slower but operate equally effectively as cues in distinguishing sounds. A group of four changes of this kind is to be found in the initial sounds of the words *yacht, what, rot* and *lot*. The word *yacht* starts with what is really a very short version of the vowel that occurs in *hid*, while *what* begins with a short version of the vowel in *hood*. In both cases there is a move towards the main vowel of the word, so that the two elements make a kind of reversed diphthong. The cue for distinguishing the first two initial sounds therefore is that Formants 1 and 2 are widely separated at the beginning of *yacht* and close together for *what*. In the second pair of words there is a glide from a lower frequency on the part of both Formants 1 and 2 and the distinction between /r/ and /l/ is one of the few for which the cue is what is happening to Formant 3. In /r/ this formant also shows a glide from a lower frequency but in /l/ there is no marked transition in Formant 3.

Practically all the acoustic cues mentioned so far have been related to frequency in some way or other. We also use a number of time cues, that is to say the brain registers the moment at which a certain change takes place and bases a decision upon this information. Time cues tend to be used for sorting sounds into rather large and general classes such as the voiced and voiceless consonants. The relation between the moment at which vocal cord vibration is switched on and the moment at which some other movement takes place is one cue of this kind. In English /b, d, g/, for example, the starting of larynx vibration tends to be very closely synchronized with the opening of the lips or the move of the tongue, while in /p, t, k/, the move of lips or tongue comes first with the vocal cords beginning to vibrate some 20 or 30 milliseconds later. A time cue of the same kind for distinguishing voiced from voiceless consonants is used when consonants follow vowels. In the two words *cab* and *cap*, the vowel is continued longer before the lips close for /b/ than before the closure for /p/; or again, in the words *bus* and *buzz*, the vowel in the first will be short and the noise will start early while in the second, the vowel is longer and the noise begins later.

It has already been said that different languages have different phoneme systems and that distinctions that are important in one language may be of no significance in another. The cues we use are dictated by the differentiations that have to be made and we shall see when we come to consider how children learn to talk, that we develop the use of cues for our mother tongue in the early years of life. If a difference is not important in the system, we do not acquire a cue for it and thus, to take up again the examples given, a Dutch or Spanish speaker has not learned a cue which will highlight the pitch difference between /s/ and /sh/, the Italian speaker does not notice the Formant 2 transition difference between *win* and *wing*, although he uses the same cue for other purposes. Similarly the English speaker has no cue to focus on the difference in the sounds representing /t/ in the words *tar* and *star*, though this difference is highly significant in many Indian and African languages. One of the examples of this kind that is particularly well-known in the English-speaking world is the fact that Japanese speakers cannot detect the difference between /r/ and /l/ sounds and cannot make the distinction when talking English. A rather endearing example is that of the Japanese who when making an after-dinner speech in English confessed that he was rather nervous and 'had butterfries in his stomach'. Since the /r–l/ distinction depends so much on the Formant 3 transition, which is not very much used for other sound differences, it is not really surprising that it should be hard to acquire for use in a foreign language.

So much emphasis has been placed on the phoneme level of operation because this is where the main ear-work of speech takes place. The patterns of intonation and rhythm are recognized in the same way but they involve a much smaller number of categories; the English system, for example, functions with six basic tones and only two rhythmic categories, formed by the strong syllables and the weaker ones. In these areas more than ever it is a matter of attending to the appropriate cues and disregarding many other variations. As far as the grammar of English is concerned, that is to say in order to recognize that a speaker is asking you a question or making a statement, is asking you to do something or telling you that you have to, has finished what he means to say or is going on, it is only necessary to notice the general outline of the intonation, rising or falling or a combination of the two. In addition to this grammatical information, however, intonation tells us a lot about the emotional attitudes of the speaker. Just as is the case with phoneme distinctions and voice quality, we are able to take in both kinds of information without letting the cues for one blur those which apply to the other. Each of us has a range of voice pitch which we tend to use in speaking quite unemotionally, simply conveying factual information, and we can sing all the tunes of English in this key. There are endless variations on these themes, however, and when we feel the slightest emotion concerning what we are talking about, the person we are talking to or the situation, we move into different keys, usually requiring a much wider range of pitch, if we are very excited even a few high Cs. If you imagine the right circumstances and say aloud first 'I simply love it' and then 'The milkman's just been', you will find the range of notes for the first is considerably wider than for the second (unless you are in love with the milkman). Some emotions, incidentally, call for a very narrow and low range of notes, as you may find out by saying with complete conviction 'It's absolutely disgusting!'. The important point is that whatever variations of this kind may be introduced, the grammatical patterns are still conveyed and are recognized by means of the same cues.

In a similar way rhythmic patterns are modified by emotional expression and words which contributed weaker syllables in an unemotional remark may be made strong. Try saying aloud the sentence '*I* don't think *I* can', putting the emphasis on the word 'I' in both cases, and you will find that this immediately conveys some emotional attitude. What emotional emphasis is not allowed to do in English is to shift the stress in a word of more than one syllable. Thus the word *enormous* has the strongest syllable in the middle and this may be emphasized to any degree in an emotional context but the stress cannot move to one of the other syllables in the word.

To sum up the ear-work of speech, then, the speech soundwaves reach the ear mechanism and result in mechanical movements which send nerve messages to the brain. There the information is organized as being relevant to acoustic cues which ensure the sorting of the incoming sounds into phoneme categories in accordance with the language system. A given cue will indicate a class of sounds and it is a combination of cues that brings about the recognition of a sound as representing a particular phoneme. Thus the presence or absence of vocal cord vibration, denoted by periodicity in the sound, at a certain moment will assign the sound to the voiced or voiceless class; a prolonged random noise may put it in the class of sounds produced by turbulence in the vocal tract; relatively low intensity might narrow the choice to /f/ or /th/ and the frequency cue supplied by formant transition lead to identification of the sound as representing the /f/ phoneme. Processes of the same kind, depending on acoustic cues, are involved in the recognition of intonation and rhythm. The ear and brain are also dealing with a great deal of non-language information relating to the speaker's personality, background, emotional outlook and so on, and in keeping with the general principle of the brain's *modus operandi*, all these things are being done at the same time.

Perhaps the hardest fact to assimilate about speech is that the activity just briefly reviewed is the whole extent of the ear's involvement in the reception of speech. We have the impression that we hear and recognize words and sentences – but we do not. We hear sounds and the brain processes them into a string of phonemes, into rhythm and intonation patterns; on the basis of these the brain reconstructs the morphemes, words and sentences of the spoken message. Indeed the process of reconstruction is very largely a matter of prediction and we shall see in the next chapter some of the principles on which this work proceeds.

6

Speech as a guessing game

> The power to guess the unseen from the seen. Henry James

Two people who have lived with each other for a good many years quite commonly find that they sometimes exchange remarks without doing any tongue- or ear-work. One knows what the other intends to say and acts accordingly and usually neither pays the matter a great deal of attention. Is this a case of the paranormal, of telepathy? We do not need to resort to such an explanation of this particular phenomenon for it happens that the couple who communicate without actually speaking are doing exactly what we all do when we are talking: they rely on knowing what to expect.

At the end of the previous chapter we said that receiving speech depends on prediction and there are circumstances in which prediction resolves itself into betting on an absolute certainty. What we say is the outcome of what we are thinking. In the case of the couple who have lived together for a long time, recurring situations and circumstances will call up habitual thoughts so that A knows what B is thinking and is about to say, not necessarily because his train of thought is the same, though it may be, but because the thought has often been expressed in speech before in that situation. This in fact is a case where the message is so certain that speech becomes unnecessary.

Prediction is one of the most powerful factors in the reception of speech. We should get nowhere at all if we did not know to some extent what to expect. This is already implied in saying that a common language is necessary for communication for we know, thanks to the memory stores in the brain, that whatever message comes in it must consist of a string of phonemes belonging to a certain inventory, that the morphemes are to be found in the list we carry in our heads, that the words are card-indexed in our dictionary and that the sentence formation will be based on routines we are familiar with. Though the variety of messages that may arrive is very great indeed, these conditions place limits upon that variation. There are a number of factors that reduce even more drastically the choice of possible elements at all levels of the language and at each succeeding moment.

Let us begin at the most general level of all. What we say depends on what we are thinking and what we are thinking depends at least partly on the situation in which we find ourselves. Even in the most scatter-brained of us there is always a train of thought, that is some sequence which is being followed. Since our remarks are the outcome of our thoughts, we are not free at any given moment to say anything in the wide world and certainly not if we want anyone else to understand what we have said. There are a whole host of things which cannot possibly be said in a particular situation, to a particular person, at a particular instant, in view of our emotional state, in view of his or her emotional state, in the presence of a third person, and so on and so on. What we say is constrained by all these factors which we might lump together and call the situation. A whole category of verbal humour is based on the momentary disregarding of constraints imposed by the situation. It is because of this element that Eliza Doolittle's 'Not bloody likely' can never fail to get a laugh.

One aspect of the limitations imposed by the situation is summed up by what we often call 'style' of speech. Familiar conversation calls for a certain style which is entirely out of place in giving a public lecture; talking to people who work for us may evoke a different style from talking to someone we work for and so on. The effects of style run through all the levels of speech and language operation; it regulates the choice of words and of grammatical construction, the pronunciation and intonation, the tempo and the loudness of the speech. As listeners we are well aware of all these constraints upon what is going to be said to us and the knowledge is an important component in knowing what to expect.

There is however a much more specific sense in which we are able to predict what is coming when we are taking in speech, a sense which refers to short-term and less general considerations. Anything that is spoken is a sequence, no matter at what level we look at it; it is a sequence of sentences, a sequence of words, of morphemes, of phonemes, of articulatory movements and of sound-waves. The essential fact about any sequence is that when any point is reached, what occurs next is dictated in part by what has gone before; it cannot be a random occurrence. It is perhaps easiest to illustrate this in the case of word sequences. The sequence of words in an English sentence may bring us to a point where it is certain what the next word is going to be, as in 'A stitch in time saves . . .'. At such a point there is a good long list of words which can be regarded as impossible, for example the word *got*. These represent the end point in a wide range of probabilities. If we look at these probabilities in terms of the odds one would be willing to bet for or against a given continuation, one would be well advised to bet pretty heavily on the continuation 'A stitch in time saves nine' and equally heavily against the continuation 'A stitch in time saves got', though notice that the odds have just been infinitesimally shortened by the fact that the sequence has now been written down. Between the certain and the impossible there lies a graded scale of probability which reflects the number of times a given continuation would be found if one surveyed the whole of English speech. A slightly different way of looking at these probabilities is to ask, with regard to every point in the sequence, how many words are there which could occur in the next position: if there is only one, this is the condition of certainty, the extreme of probability; if there were three, then the probability for each of them is high; if there were twenty, the probability for each one is lower and if there were a hundred, the probability for each would be very low.

It was Claude Shannon, one of the originators of information theory, who first pointed out and demonstrated that, incredible as it may seem, the brain is equipped to compute these probabilities, which of course alter at every point in the sequence.

The technique he used was a kind of guessing game played in this way. Supposing we take the first four words of some piece of English that has actually occurred; we give these to an English speaker and ask him to guess what the fifth word might be. We leave his suggested word in the sequence, take away the first word and then get another person to suggest the next word. By repeating the operation again and again we can build up a continuous passage which reflects the computation of probabilities based on sequences of four words. The same process can be carried out giving the person who is guessing only one word, or ten words or fifteen words and so on, or of course we can get a random sequence of words by giving no word to start with. The more words we supply, the nearer the result will come to being a normal English sequence. Here are a few examples obtained in this way, beginning with one in which there is no connection, except a chance one, between each word and the next:

> trimmer to like forget did eating she hardly and me making them the on said catalogue looked or mother almost they animals clear you buy . . .

Now a sequence where one word has been given, so that every two words are linked as they would be in normal English:

> The camera shop and boyhood friend from fish and screamed loudly men only when seen again and then it was jumping in the tree is idiotic . . .

The next begins to sound rather closer to normal because each successive sequence of six words is linked by normal probabilities:

> I have a few little facts here to test that needs a lot of time for studying and praying for guidance in living in accordance with common ideas . . .

Finally here is a passage in which normal probabilities are maintained over a string of fifteen words:

> The very next day they went for a picnic in the woods which they thought would be suitable for them to visit

> although they saw bulls in the field which might attack the girls savagely and so cause them untold fear no harm whatever will come providing that they flee all possible dangers arising from the long since completed series of adventures they began last week on work which took them far too far away . . .

When we follow anything that is said to us, we are applying our knowledge of the probabilities all the time and we expect that these probabilities will not be contradicted by what comes in, as they are by all the passages just given. The interesting point is that we do notice the disjointedness even in the last passage. This is partly because when people are asked to suggest a continuation, they do not very readily think of ending a clause or a sentence whereas normal sequences require that this should occur.

It is not only the words in the spoken message that are linked in this way but all the other language elements, including the phonemes. Because the phonemes are essentially the sound elements of the system it is difficult to discuss them very fully on the printed page unless one has a letter available for each phoneme; as we said earlier, this is why a forty-letter alphabet has been devised for English in connection with reading difficulties. What has happened in English is that the spelling has been more or less frozen for the best part of three hundred years while the sounds of our speech and hence the phoneme system have been undergoing a number of changes, giving rise to the well-known anomalies of English spelling of the *rough, dough, through, hiccough* variety. For the present purpose all the basic facts can be illustrated with the ordinary alphabet which is after all a way of representing the phonemes in the system. The fact that phonemes follow each other in the sequence with varying degrees of probability is adequately reflected by the fact that letters do the same and the guessing game technique can be applied in a slightly different form to letters. Just as any spoken message in English is a sequence of phonemes each taken from the complete list of forty, so any written message will be a sequence taken from the twenty-six letters of the alphabet. The succession of letters is governed by the laws of probability for ordinary English and you can demonstrate the effect by getting any willing victim to do the guessing. First select a complete English sentence, which is not of course revealed to the person guessing, and then ask him what the first letter is. He should keep some record of his guesses so that he does not suggest the same letter twice, and you tell him each time his guess is wrong. In these conditions his twenty-sixth guess must in any case bring him to the right letter but he is unlikely to need anything like this number before he guesses correctly for the first position in the sentence. When he does so, he needs to write down the letter because he is going to build up the whole sentence letter by letter; on your side the interest is in keeping account of the total number of guesses needed at each position in the sentence. Let us say that the first letter in the sequence is actually *y*, and he may well take 12 or 15 guesses to reach the right answer. When he now goes on to guess at the second position, he applies his very extensive knowledge of the English language system, so when he searches round in his brain for possible continuations of the sequence, he very soon realizes that the only candidates are the vowel letters *a, e, i, o, u*. The maximum number of guesses he will use here is therefore five and as the letters are not equally likely he will probably guess correctly at the first or second guess. The correct guess is actually *yo*. At this point it would be very surprising if the person did not make his first guess *u* for the next position, and this is correct, so in the course of only three positions in the sentence the number of guesses has dropped from 12 to 2 to 1, showing that the constraint on the possible choice of letters has become more stringent. Obviously the person guessing is trying all the time to complete words that are probable in the context and at the beginning of the sentence he will be looking for a common word that may come first in a sentence; hence his first shot in the third place will aim to complete the word *you* rather than lead to such outsiders as *yodel, yoga, yoicks* or even *yonder*. As he goes on through the sentence, his guesses will always be regulated by efforts to make sense of the message, that is by the links between words. The further he gets into the sentence, the more the possible word choices are reduced and with them the letter choices. Within words also the constraints become stronger as the word proceeds so there will generally be some increase in the number of guesses at the beginning of each fresh word. All the time the object is to build a sensible and probable message. If the sentence were, for example, 'You don't have to be here till eight', there will be several points where the number of guesses will be quite high and other stretches where the first guess will give the right answer in successive positions. Let us imagine the person guessing has reached the end of the word *till*. He will certainly think it possible that some hour is going to be named; there are just five initial letters for the possible numbers. There is no evidence in the preceding sequence to favour one number rather than another so there is a 20 per cent chance of each being the correct one. When he finds that the right letter is *e*, however, the next letter has to be one of two, either *i* or *l*, and when this is settled as *i*, he must get *g*, *h*, *t* all at the first guess.

All the operations that have been exemplified here with letters can be done with phonemes, though in order actually to play the guessing game in this way we have to find someone who is overtly aware that he knows the phoneme system of English and is able to write down the list, as it were. The essential point is that the brain carries this kind of information about the language in addition to the stores and routines that have already been mentioned and it literally does the appropriate statistical calculations, for that is what they amount to, when it is reconstructing the incoming message. As soon as the sounds of speech arrive at the ear, the brain applies to them the criteria formed by the acoustic cues and begins to build up a string of phonemes. At once it starts to predict the continuation of the message at the phoneme level, using its computed probabilities, and converts phoneme strings into morpheme and word sequences, having regard to the probabilities at each of these levels too. These operations are all going on at the same time when we take in speech and consequently the word predicted as the most probable continuation decides what we expect to occur next at the morpheme and phoneme levels; what turns up in the continuing sound input determines the predictions at the other levels, and so the process goes on. Not infrequently the sounds, when converted into a phoneme sequence, contradict the predictions at the word level, for example, and then there has to be a swift revision of the calculations and a new prediction at all the levels. Sometimes there is a very long lag before the predictions are seen to be wrong and this leads to a string of errors which nonetheless make a perfectly sensible message. This is the basis of the game sometimes played at children's parties which consists in starting a whispered message at some point in a large circle of children and seeing just what distortions have overtaken the message by the time it has got back to the same point, a game sometimes known as 'Russian Whispers', perhaps because the sibilant twittering to which it gives rise bears some resemblance to the sound of spoken Russian. An example of the same effect is the classic from a long past war in which it is asserted that a message left one military post in the form 'Send reinforcements: I am going to advance' and arrived at another military post in the form 'Send three and fourpence: I am going to a dance'. All the internal probabilities are maintained in the second version; only the situation might argue against it.

It now becomes clearer in what sense we actually hear nothing but the sounds that yield the phoneme string (and of course the rhythm and intonation patterns). Everything else is constructed from the phoneme sequence in the listener's brain, with continual checking back to the sounds in order to confirm the predictions and constructions. The influence of sequential probability is so powerful at the word and morpheme levels that quite a degree of uncertainty can be tolerated at the phoneme level. This again can be illustrated in the parallel of printed English. In the following passage every fourth letter is missing but the text remains perfectly readable:

> Spe–ch m–kes –se o– par–s of –he b–dy w–ich –re p–ima–ily –evo–ed t– oth–r fu–cti–ns: b–eat–ing, –hew–ng, s–all–win–. The –rga– of h–ari–g se–ves –o

ot–er p–rpo–e bu– as w– hav– see– it i– clo–ely –onn-cte– wit– the –rga– of b–lan–e.

The technical term for the feature in language that makes it possible to predict elements in a sequence is *redundancy*. All natural languages that we know anything about exhibit a high degree of redundancy. The word can be applied equally well in its everyday sense to mean that any message contains much more information than is really needed in order to take in its contents. In the text printed above 25 per cent of the letters have been replaced by a sign which tells us only that a letter stood in that position and not which of the twenty-six letters it was. Yet we can read the message without this considerable fraction of the total information. The same fact is conveyed by the result of the guessing game because any letter guessed at the first guess could certainly be replaced by some neutral sign.

Exactly the same situation holds when we are dealing with the phoneme sequence of a spoken message, though it is hard to exemplify the effect satisfactorily on the printed page. The fact remains that the phoneme string could be as full of blanks as the printed passage above and we should still understand the whole of the spoken message. What we have to get from the sound-waves is enough information to build the scaffolding of the remark, as it were, and then the brain will complete the entire language structure with no trouble at all. In other words, we do not need to hear everything that is said because a good deal of the time we know what it must be. Very roughly speaking, if we actually hear about half of what is said to us in English, we can guess the rest quite successfully. If we are injudicious enough to listen to a political speech, of course, then 10 per cent is probably enough. This is a basic fact about the reception of speech and if you find it particularly hard to swallow, you can with a little ingenuity find experiments to try out on your friends and acquaintances. In the right circumstances you can ask someone to give you a 'tlean dlass' and, provided you have practised a bit so as not to make too much of a splash about it, no one will ever know that you did not say 'clean glass' because this is obviously what the sequence demands. Or if you say to someone that you have just been talking to a fellow who is a cytologist, the odds are certainly 99 to 1 that he will think the man was a psychologist. Again the brain has reconstructed a message based on reasonable predictions.

In both of these examples we cannot say that the listener *hears* /k/, for the cues in the actual sound-waves are inappropriate. The brain has simply reconstructed a plausible message on the framework of what it has heard. In the first case it arrived at the right conclusion, that is it corrected the errors in the input; in the second it made a mistake, but that mistake is almost certain to be corrected very rapidly in the course of conversation. A few more remarks and it will become clear to the listener that the person referred to is someone who is concerned with the study of cells and not one who deals with the mental activities of human beings (and rats!).

One of the most remarkable features of communication by speech is the provision that it makes for correcting errors. The errors by the way are very infrequent indeed; we notice them when they occur and never realize how many millions of words are exchanged without any mistake. It is the redundancy of language which ensures that messages can be taken in even when there is a great deal of noise or distortion of the sound-waves and which also ensures that when an error is made, it is corrected within quite a short time. All of us make mistakes occasionally when we are talking and we may make them too when we are listening. If the speaker makes an error, he himself will usually realize it almost immediately and will go back and correct it. Whether he does so or not, the listener corrects the mistake in taking in the message because his reconstruction of it tells him what the correct version must be. The kind of mistake from the speaker that we are most familiar with is the spoonerism, named after the Reverend Dr Spooner, an Oxford don who was evidently unusually prone to the type of speech error which consists in transposing sounds, especially the initial ones of words. Surprisingly enough Dr Spooner died as recently as 1930 and in any case one can be sure that the phenomenon existed long before his day. A number of examples attributed to him have become so well-known as scarcely to call for repetition, things like his announcing a hymn title as 'Kingquering congs their takels tight', or his expressing 'a half-warmed fish' and assuring someone 'the verger will sew you into a sheet'. Inevitably a host of apocryphal anecdotes grow up round such a character, among them the following, which is interesting because it concerns not really the transposing of sounds but a confusion at the level of the meaning of words. Dr Spooner is reported to have gone into one of the more expensive opticians' shops in Wigmore Street in London and to have approached the elegant young man behind the counter with the question 'Can you let me have a signifying glass?' 'A what, sir?' replied the puzzled young man. 'A signifying glass'. Still at a loss, the young man said 'I'm afraid not, sir', to which the Reverend Doctor replied 'Ah well, it don't magnify'. This clearly cannot be authentic because the initial error is only possible if the speaker's brain is quite certain that the article will be refused, thereby calling up the expression 'It don't signify', but it serves to illustrate the essential nature of such errors. They are produced by the fact that the brain is dealing with several different levels of the message at the same time, as we saw earlier, and the arrangements already made at one level may interfere with the sequence of events at another. In the typical spoonerism, the string of phonemes is planned in advance of the point which has been reached by the muscle movements and so a particular instruction to the muscles gets put in ahead of the point where it is appropriate. It is a natural reaction to balance this by a transposition of sounds. By listening to people who are talking in public or on the radio or television one can collect any number of examples. They tend to turn up in these conditions because the speaker's thinking is usually even further ahead of his tongue than in ordinary conversation. In the days when radio announcers read the weather reports themselves, one informed his listeners that it had been 'a gay of dales'. When his tongue got to the point of producing *day*, his brain had already set up the phoneme string beyond the word *gales* and the initial /g/ was injected into the movement for *day*, with a consequent compensation when the word *gales* itself was reached. These errors are not confined to the initial sounds in words, nor indeed to the consonant sounds, as we see from examples such as 'I'll curve the tarkey' or an enquiry as to the way to 'Sorrey Ducks' in London.

Speech errors have considerable significance because they reveal a great deal about the working of the brain during speech. So long as all goes smoothly there is not much to show what it is doing in the way of language organization when someone is talking, but when a mistake is made we can often see from the error that the brain must be operating in a particular way. It was suggested that in 'a gay of dales' the string of phonemes already organized by the brain was responsible for the mistake, but one might equally well think that the speaker's brain had drawn the wrong word out of the dictionary in each case, since both are English words. This is very unlikely for a reason which we shall see in a moment, but other examples demonstrate that this is not what is happening. A spoonerism like 'an estape of skeam' cannot be accounted for on the dictionary level because, although the word *scheme* exists, there is no English word *estape*. Spoonerisms really are errors that arise at the level of the phoneme string. We refer to them as slips of the tongue but they are actually slips of the brain.

It might at first seem a strange idea that when we are talking our brain is busy putting together the grammatical bits of the message. One might suppose that at most complete words would be assembled in the right order, but a certain kind of error that occurs repeatedly shows that at one level we do indeed arrange the morphemes in the required sequence and that it is possible for these elements to get detached and to appear in the wrong place. In a mistake like 'We've loved to learn mountains', the words *learn* and *love* have become transposed but the *-d* that marks the past tense is still in the right place, independently of the word to which it belongs grammatically. If the mistake were bound to affect a whole word, then the sentence would have been 'We've love to learned mountains', a kind of error which is never heard. These grammatical bits of the language can be displaced in the most bizarre sort of way. A professor giving a public lecture was heard to embark on a remark which began 'This is as un-yet . . .'. He realized immediately that something was awry, so he started again; once more he said 'This is as un-yet . . . and it was not until the third attempt that he sorted things out and incidentally revealed the source of the error by saying 'This is an as yet unsolved problem'. The part of his brain that was stringing together the grammatical bits had got ahead to the word *unsolved* from which the morpheme *un-* became detached and inserted in advance of its proper place. A moment's lapse had left him doubtful whether he intended to say 'This is as yet an unsolved problem' or to use the more awkward construction that he eventually came out with 'This is an as yet unsolved problem'. Such mistakes could not occur unless at some stage the brain were really arranging the string of grammatical elements and they often arise where the speaker is undecided between two possible ways of saying a thing. One very odd example came from a speaker who began 'Fancy his thoughting . . .'. This really means that he was oscillating between 'Fancy his thinking . . .' and 'Fancy, he thought . . .'. In the majority of cases speakers correct themselves either at once or after a short interval but sometimes they do not notice that they have made a mistake and then the listener inserts his own correction, as for instance when a speaker relating an incident at a railway station referred to the 'ticking-office clerk'.

Errors can certainly occur which lead to the misplacing of whole words, but they affect the meaning of the remark and do not give rise to the spoonerisms we were considering earlier. When a word gets out of place we tend to stop and start again or we may do our best to modify the course of what we are saying in order to preserve the sense of what we wanted to convey. A good example of this kind was provided by a speaker who corrected himself in a second attempt and said 'Unfortunately it's against Leigh's will'. What he had said first, however, was 'Unfortunately it's against Will's desire'. No such person as *Will* was concerned in the matter at all, but the word *will* had got into the message ahead of its proper place and so the speaker had had to find some other word to convey the same meaning; his brain came up with the word *desire*, in this way preserving the general sense of the remark but of course upsetting the reference to the person in question, so that the correction had in the end to be made. This is a case where the meaning of the word had intruded before its time so that some adjustment had to be resorted to unless the sentence were going to be abandoned altogether. The brain in organizing the sense of the message has again run ahead of the actual word selection.

A speaker's mistakes are due then to the fact that many processes are going on in his brain during the moments that precede the articulation of the sounds. His ear is continually monitoring the speech he is sending out and for the most part it confirms that what is spoken is what is intended, but very occasionally there is a discrepancy and then the whole system is alerted and generally brought to a stop. A parallel can be seen in typewriting where the eye is reading the output from the fingers; when it sees some sequence like *srtong*, for example, it reports it to the brain and the hands are arrested in order that the mistake may be corrected. The error has arisen because the brain has given the wrong instructions to the fingers and not because the brain intended to put out the sequence *srtong* any more than the radio announcer meant to say 'a gay of dales'.

Errors in speaking and listening are comparatively rare and the reason why they practically never upset communication lies in the redundancy which has been the main topic of this chapter. It was Norbert Wiener, the man who invented the word 'cybernetics', who said that the most important thing you can know about a message is that it makes sense. Listeners are always bringing to bear their knowledge of the language system and its statistics in order to make sense of what they hear. They reconstruct and predict as the message continues and if an error occurs they correct it because they know what the message 'must be'. The correction does not always happen immediately; we are all familiar with the sensation of going back to a particular point, perhaps after a few seconds, and straightening out what has been said. The interval may be very much longer than this, a matter of hours or even days, before the thought comes into our minds 'He must have said so-and-so'.

A vital part of knowing a language therefore is this capacity for knowing what to expect. The early years of practice in our mother tongue give us our acquaintance with the necessary statistics and we know what sweat, blood and tears are needed if we want to reach anything like the same level of operation in a foreign language. We use the capacity every time we talk, even in face-to-face conversation, and when conditions get difficult we rely more and more on our ability to guess. The ordinary line telephone, for example, supplies us with something less than half the range of frequencies we receive when in the same room with someone. The telephone system would not work at all if we could not guess successfully, but as it is we do not encounter much difficulty except with things like proper names, where redundancy does not help us very much. In the course of a telephone conversation someone might say to you 'Oh, by the way, I saw old Haythornthwaite a few days ago'. If the name is not one you are very familiar with, we all know the kind of exchange that follows, leading into 'H for Harry, A for Apple, Y for York, T for Tommy, H for Harry, O for Orange' and at that point you probably exclaim 'Oh, you mean Haythornthwaite' because redundancy has taken over once more and you know what the end of the sequence must be. So talking to each other really is largely a guessing game in which fortunately we do know most of the answers.

7

Speech servo-mechanisms

> **Oh, many a shaft at random sent**
> **Finds mark the archer little meant.** Walter Scott

Although the more loquacious among our acquaintances may sometimes incline us to doubt the fact, it is clear that no one was ever born talking. The movements we make in speech have been learned through hours, days and years of practice and it is this that makes us able to carry them on with the very small amount of attention that we normally pay to them. Speech movements are actually the most finely co-ordinated, the most accurately timed and the most closely controlled voluntary movements that a human being ever makes. This may be hard to believe when we think of the performance of a virtuoso in any field such as music or sport, which demands feats of co-ordination and miracles of timing which are beyond the reach of most of us. The pianist who plays the 'Emperor' concerto, the tennis player who wins a championship, the gymnast who wins a gold medal, all operate at a very high level of skill, yet the movements they make do not compare with those which every one of us makes when we are talking. In the action of the speech mechanism, distances are measured in millimetres, time differences in milliseconds and the operation is so complex that hundreds of muscles have to be controlled. Wherever such a fine degree of control is achieved, whether in nature or in man-made devices, we find that the systems involved share a common feature, usually referred to as *feedback*.

A boy throwing a ball uses his arm muscles to set the ball moving in a certain direction, but however much attention he may devote to the task right up to the last moment, once the ball has left his hand, he has no further control over its flight, a matter of some regret of course if an error of judgment has sent it through a neighbour's window. This is an arrangement in which a train of events is set going and is allowed to run its inevitable course; the boy's brain decides to throw the ball, it instructs the arm and hand muscles, the ball leaves the hand and pursues a course determined by the laws of physics. A parallel case but carried out in slow motion, as it were, is the game sometimes played at parties for small children of pinning the tail on the donkey; a child is blindfolded, takes the tail with its pin in his hand and has a shot at placing it in the right place on the donkey's body. Of course the game would not be a game at all if the child were not blindfold. This would change the system entirely and would in fact introduce feedback. If the child could see, then the movement of his hand would be controlled on the basis of information coming in from his eyes. The first step would consist in the brain instructing the arm to bring the hand nearer to the donkey; the eyes would see both the tail and the target position on the donkey and would report to the brain, let us say, 'Too far to the right'. Brain then tells the arm to move the hand nearer and to the left; eyes now report 'Tail is nearer to the donkey and about two inches to the left of the target'. Because of the information fed back to the brain by the eyes, there is continual correction of the movement of the tail until at last it is placed in the target position. The essence of feedback control then is that the activity of the system, in this case the brain and arm, is continuously modified by the effects of that activity; vision here forms a feedback loop. For centuries firearms and other offensive weapons operated on the ballistic principle of the boy who throws the ball; in the last decades, feedback control has been introduced into this area by the employment of servo-mechanisms, for example in the guided missile whose path is continuously controlled by its 'perception' of the heat emitted by the target.

The very close control which we exercise over our movements when we are talking is effected by means of a number of feedbacks. Their most important function is to regulate the timing of the various muscle actions which, as we saw in a

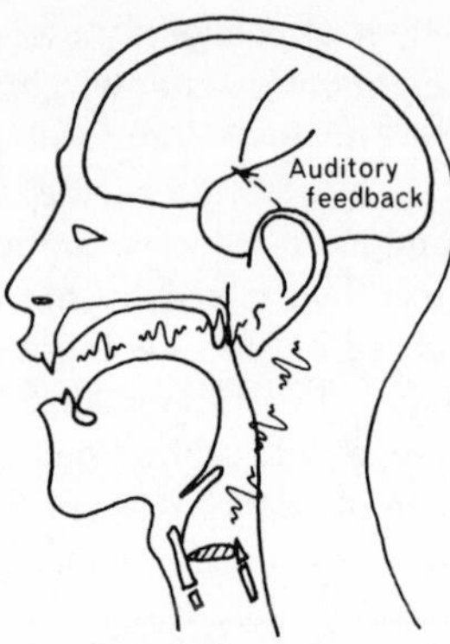

Speech sound-waves travelling through the bones and tissues of the skull reach the ear and provide auditory feedback to the brain where the information is used in the control of speech movements.

previous chapter, implement the complex distinctions which the language system demands. A difference of some ten or twenty milliseconds in the moment at which larynx vibration is switched on, for example, will make the distinction between the cue for a voiced or a voiceless consonant, as in *pit* and *bit*. The tongue and soft palate, although relatively slow-moving, have to move in accordance with a very precise time scheme; both of them are involved, together with larynx switching, in conveying the difference between *bend* and *bent* and some very subtle timing of tongue action is needed merely to utter a word like *splash* or *risks*. In all ordinary circumstances the brain regulates the timing of speech movements with the help of *auditory feedback*. The speaker's brain issues instructions to the muscles to start up certain actions or movements and it receives in return a continuous flow of information about the sounds that are being produced, since these sounds reach the ear of the speaker as well as the ears of the listeners. The ear and its connections with the brain make up the auditory feedback loop in speech. In a word like *risks*, for example, auditory feedback tells the brain when the vowel sound has continued for just the right amount of time so that the instruction can be given to make a rapid movement of the tongue for /s/, at the same time switching off the larynx vibrations and increasing the amount of air flowing through the mouth. When this hissing sound has been relayed to the brain for the appropriate time, the order is given for another rapid move of the back of the tongue which interposes a short silence; the silence is registered by the brain and when it has lasted long enough, the hissing sound is started again by a repetition of the previous actions. As in this example, it is generally the sound of our own speech that is used by the brain in the accurate timing of very complex speech movements.

Articulation is not of course simply a matter of timing but of distances that have to be covered in the given time. If you try saying aloud first of all *the risks* and then *the disks*, you will realize that the movements are remarkably similar, though we hear the difference in the sounds easily enough. In fact the tongue moves a greater distance in a shorter time in the second than it does in the first and this change in pace is a vital feature of the articulation. Small differences in distance and in rate of movement are judged with the help of auditory feedback which in the normal course of events deals with them without any difficulty. It is interesting, though, that tongue-twisters depend for their success on the stringing together of sounds which call for small differences in articulation which after a few repetitions cause complete confusion in the circuit formed by the auditory feedback and the outgoing commands to the muscles. Why is it difficult to get even once through a nonsense like 'The sea seetheth and it suffiseth us'? The differences in movement for /s/, /f/ and /th/ are rather small so that when all three turn up in varying succession in a short space of time, the control system tends to break down. All tongue-twisters rely on this feature: the nasal consonants /m, n, ng/ are the basis in 'Sitting on the balcony, hiccoughing amicably, welcoming them in' which becomes really difficult only in the last stretch where all three nasals are in close proximity. Even an apparently innocuous alternation like 'red leather, yellow leather' if repeated often enough will lead at the least to something like 'red yellow, leather leather' because of the articulatory similarities. Such sequences are of course artificial and do not generally arise in spontaneous speech, but we do run into them occasionally in conversation and when we do, they cause slight problems of control which are manifested in errors and repetitions.

Mention has already been made of one aspect of auditory feedback in speech in connection with the effect of noise on the loudness of our speech. It is our ears which tell us when the balance between the loudness of our own speech and that of any noise that may be going on is something less than satisfactory; auditory feedback enables us to judge how much we must raise our voice in order to restore the balance.

One interesting and important fact about auditory feedback concerns the nature of the pathway by which we hear our own speech. In these days of the ubiquitous tape-recorder there are a very large number of people who have heard the sound of their own voice coming from a recording machine; among them it is very doubtful if there is a single one who, upon having this experience for the first time, immediately recognized the voice as being his own. This means that the version we hear of our own speech is markedly different from what other people hear. Why is this? The whole of our sound-producing mechanism for speech is in our head and so too is the hearing mechanism. Practically all of what we hear of our own speech travels to our ears through the bones and tissues of our skull and very little of it actually returns from the surrounding air. This acoustic pathway through the head substantially modifies the sound-waves of our speech, materially altering the relative loudness of high and low frequencies, so that we receive an absolutely unique version of the sound, one that is higher and lighter in quality than the version heard by other people. We have as it were a completely private telephone line from our speech mechanism to our brain; it brings us an impression of our speech which is shared by no one else in the world. In order that we should hear our speech as others hear it, it has to be picked up by a microphone and recorded. The discrepancy between the private and the public version of our speech is so great that not only do we not recognize the public one on first hearing, but no matter how many times we hear our voice recorded, we always retain some impression that it is only 'the one they say is me'.

The strongest evidence for the importance of auditory feedback in the control of speech movements comes from a particular trick that can be played with the help of a suitable tape-recorder. If you were talking into a microphone and your speech were amplified and led to a pair of earphones which you were wearing, you would then be hearing the public version of your speech, since it had been picked up from the surrounding air. These sounds could be made loud enough to drown more or less completely the private version, which is of course still reaching your ears. Imagine now that the microphone leads to a tape-recorder and that your speech is being continuously recorded, and that what comes into your earphones is the speech replayed from the tape. The replaying of the tape cannot be simultaneous with the recording so that there is a time interval between the movements of the speech mechanism and the feeding back of the sound to your ears. This effect is referred to as *delayed auditory feedback* and it usually has a most dramatic effect on people's speech. When a delay is introduced, most speakers begin to stammer and if they are particularly susceptible, their speech movements become so disrupted that they stop talking altogether. Why should this happen? In normal circumstances the brain initiates a particular speech movement and judges the right moment for the next one on the basis of the sound which is fed back to it. If there is a delay in the auditory feedback, this sound does not arrive at the moment when it is expected and so the sequence of movements is interfered with and generally one of two things will happen. If the sound is one which can be prolonged, such as a vowel or a /sh/ for example, the speaker will simply keep the sound going until the fed back sound eventually arrives and will then proceed to the next movement. Some sounds cannot be treated in this way, however, because they require a rapid movement followed by a silence, or vice versa, and in these cases the speaker will tend to repeat the movement until the delay is past and the sound arrives. A syllable beginning with /p/, /t/ or /k/, for instance, may be repeated a number of times much in the way that some stammerers are apt to do. The general effect therefore is very much like that of a stammer (see p. 147), with continual lengthening and repetition of sounds. People vary considerably in their susceptibility to the effect of delayed auditory feedback; the maximum disruption of speech is usually obtained with delays of about one-tenth to one-fifth of a second and naturally rather sophisticated equipment is needed to produce this. If you own a tape-recorder which will allow you to replay the tape while the machine is in the record position, however, you can probably get some idea of the sensation. You need to talk into the recording microphone while listening to the tape replay through a pair of earphones at a fairly high level. It is necessary to use earphones so as to get the speech loud enough without setting up a howl in the loudspeaker, which incidentally is due to acoustic feedback from loudspeaker to microphone. If you have a choice of tape speed, you will probably need to use the highest available.

Delayed auditory feedback would not have this effect on speech movements unless auditory feedback were in use in the normal course of events. What is happening is that false information is being returned to the brain and this upsets the control system. Auditory feedback can be put out of action for example by the onset of deafness; if this happens suddenly in middle life, usually the production of speech as well as its reception is affected. It can also be obliterated temporarily if we are surrounded by very loud noise, like that set up by a very noisy tube train or a nearby jet engine or pneumatic drill. We noticed earlier that when we talk in a noise we do our best to raise our voice above the noise level, but we may reach a point where this is no longer possible, and we say we cannot hear ourselves speak or cannot hear ourselves think, which is a good pointer to the brain work involved in speech. In fact we can continue to talk in these conditions and apart from the effort which it costs us, the movements are not very much affected. If auditory feedback is so important, how is it possible for us to talk in a very loud noise?

The answer is to be found in the second feedback loop which

operates all the time we are talking, for we do not depend exclusively on the auditory feedback loop. The muscles which we use for all our voluntary movements have a two-way connection to the brain. There are the nerves which carry instructions from the brain to the muscle fibres but there are also nerves going from the muscles to the brain which relay information as to the state of the muscle at succeeding moments. The latter constitute the kinaesthetic feedback, giving the feeling of movement, and the brain relies very heavily on this feedback loop for the regulation of all voluntary movements. When we are walking along, our foot, leg and thigh muscles are busy relaying information to the brain as to what they are doing and the amount of effort they are putting out; it is with the help of this fed back information that the brain keeps the activity running smoothly. Other feedbacks are available when we are walking. If we are wise we usually look where we are going, that is to say visual feedback is at our disposal, but in the normal way we do not look down at our feet all the time in order that the brain should be able to tell the legs to put the left foot forward a certain distance and then to follow this with the right. When we go upstairs or step up a kerb, however, we bring in visual feedback as a matter of course.

The patterns of muscle action for all our habitual movements are held in memory stores in the brain as a result of the immense amount of practice which went into the learning of them. These kinaesthetic patterns which form our motor memory make it possible for the brain to plan the movements before they are carried out; it knows in advance just how much muscle effort to command for a given purpose. Most of the time the kinaesthetic feedback loop returns the information that the movements are going according to plan but occasionally there is an exception. If we run upstairs in the dark, we cannot use visual feedback and have to rely on kinaesthetic feedback. Everyone knows the sensation when we think that there is one more step at the top of the stairs and it turns out there is not. The brain tells the muscles to raise the weight of the body another eight inches, to put down the right foot on the higher level and to follow it by the left foot; this time, however, the plan is not matched by the circumstances and the result is rather disastrous. Notice that though we may stumble, we do not usually fall flat on our face; in the light of the information fed back to it, the brain makes a lightning change of plan so that the feet, legs and torso can cope with the unexpected situation. A similar example is the case where we go to pick up something like a suitcase or a kettle which we believe to be heavy and it turns out that it is light, the suitcase empty or the kettle unfilled. In either case the planned muscle effort is very nicely adjusted to the weight to be lifted in anticipation; because of the mismatch between the plan and the reality, the thing flies in the air.

The subtlety with which the brain matches the effort to the task is almost incredible. Imagine what is happening when you travel upwards in a fairly fast moving lift. If you are at all used to the particular lift, you experience no marked sensation because your muscles put out a smoothly changing amount of effort in order to counteract exactly the acceleration as you leave the lower level and in reverse compensates for the deceleration as you reach the top. Kinaesthetic feedback is the basis for this miraculously smooth matching of effort to the load. If the lift is a public one such as are still in use in some London tube stations, you will almost certainly be in the company of someone who is not used to riding in the lift and who betrays by shudders, sighs and exclamations that they are not equal to the job of counteracting the acceleration and deceleration.

All our habitual movements, walking, running, cleaning our teeth, using a knife and fork, riding a bicycle, driving a car, are regulated by this kinaesthetic system, in some circumstances aided by other feedback loops. The act of writing, for example, is carried on mainly on the basis of kinaesthetic feedback but with the help normally of visual feedback. It is the eyes that tell our brain when we are writing an *a* exactly how far to go in one direction and when to reverse. We can however write in the dark or with our eyes shut because kinaesthetic feedback by itself can keep the movements going; the writing inevitably looks somewhat different, particularly

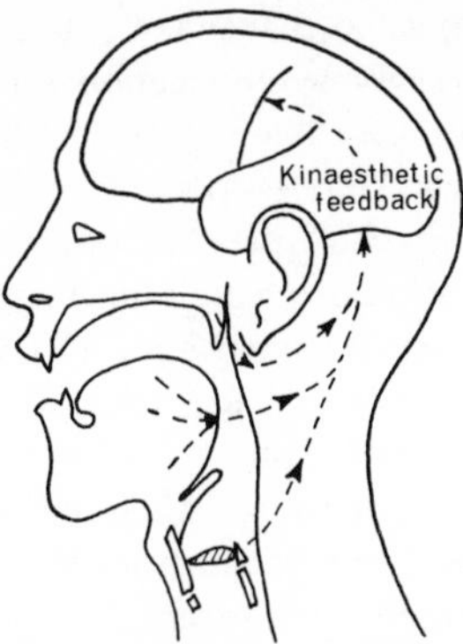

Information from all the muscles used in speaking is sent back to the brain and provides the kinaesthetic feedback necessary for the control of speech movements.

in matters of spacing, regularity and alignment, all of which are usually controlled through visual feedback.

Just as the movements of writing depend on visual and kinaesthetic feedback, so the movements of speech depend on both auditory and kinaesthetic feedback. While we are talking the brain gets news about the sounds that are being generated and also about the muscle actions at the same time. An utterance is based on a kinaesthetic plan which is expected to produce acoustic results. If, as we saw in the case of delayed auditory feedback, the acoustic result does not appear to match the plan, then there is trouble with the control system; if, on the other hand, the auditory feedback is temporarily put out of action by a loud noise so that it gives no information at all, then the movements can continue on the basis of the kinaesthetic feedback. We shall see in the next chapter that when we are learning to talk, the auditory feedback is a vital component, but once we have learned, we can keep going at least for a time without hearing the sounds.

There is one further feedback that plays some part in speech and that is the tactual feedback, which is not to be confused with the kinaesthetic. We have quite an acute sense of touch over a good portion of the tongue's surface, on the inside of the lips and the gums, so that when contact is made in these places, the brain receives information about speech movements through tactual feedback. This feedback loop does not seem in normal circumstances to play anything like as important a role in the control of speech as the auditory and kinaesthetic feedbacks, but it does have some influence on speech as most of us know from the experience of having a local anaesthetic at the dentist's; we do feel that our speech is affected until the anaesthesia wears off.

These three feedback loops then constitute the servomechanism of speech and make possible the control of the immensely complex muscle systems, the accurate timing of their action and the high degree of co-ordination which speech demands. Thanks to these mechanisms, we all perform miracles of timing and control which are not accessible to many an able pianist in his own sphere.

8

How did we learn to do it?

'Tis nature's plan
The child should grow into the man. — Longfellow

If there is one thing that is more astonishing than the ability of the adult human being to talk it is the process by which he learns to do this. Some parts of this process are still very much a sealed book but it is at least possible to describe what the child is doing at various stages in his development of speech even if we do not know exactly how he manages to learn to do it. From the very first moments of his life on earth a baby makes sounds, but for some time they are rather far removed from articulate speech. In something like a year he will probably be at the point where /dada/ will represent the peak of his achievement as a speaker; one more year and he will be coming out with remarks like 'all-gone milk' and after this it seems no time at all before he is capable of saying 'You know, Mummy, this one isn't as nice as the green one Daddy gave me yesterday'. This is a truly remarkable feat of learning and yet it is one that is performed by the vast majority of human beings. We have seen in previous chapters some of the complex operations that are involved in dealing with speech and language and it has been stressed a number of times that the key to the process lies in brain-work, though of course tongue-work and ear-work also play a part. In this chapter we shall see how much can be said about the ways in which the child's brain develops the requisite capacity, how the memory stores are amassed and how the necessary practice by the tongue and ear is carried out.

In the first few weeks of life most babies are fairly quiet except when they happen to be crying. Any mother can tell you why babies cry: it is because they are uncomfortable or unhappy in some way – they are hungry, or have a pain, or have been suddenly disturbed or need changing. The cry just means that the baby is getting unpleasant sensations of one sort or another and wants something done about it. In a particular baby the cry does not vary a great deal except in its persistence perhaps, but a mother soon learns to recognize the cry of her own child. The crying is important from the point of view of speech because the larynx is already being used to generate sound and because the pattern of breathing for speech is being established. When the baby is quiet, his breathing is a rhythmical 'in-out' but when he begins to cry this is all changed. Sometimes a single cry will go on and on until one wonders how the baby can possibly keep it up without bursting something; then there is a break while he takes in more air, only to start all over again. Already at this early stage it is the air coming from the lungs that is used to produce sound at the larynx, though one will sometimes hear babies also making sound as the air goes in.

It is not very long however before the baby begins to make another kind of sound, one that indicates that life is going rather well and things are particularly pleasant. These sounds of pleasure are the cooings and gurglings which usually come along round about the age of three months and which give so much satisfaction to mummy, making the broken nights and sleepless mornings so well worth while. The breathing pattern for the pleasure sounds is similar to that for the crying but their quality is quite different and in fact the vocal tract is beginning to have more influence on what comes out of the mouth, for the sound of crying is not much modified by its passage through the vocal tract.

In this first period of his life, the baby not only sends out his own sounds of displeasure and pleasure, but he very soon begins to notice some of the sounds that are going on around him. He associates his mother's voice with pleasant things like feeding and bathing and being picked up and after a short time he will respond to the voice itself, especially to the tone of voice, by smiling. This is an important factor because it links all the things which are of interest to the baby with speech and the ordinary mother is quite right in following her instinct to talk to her baby while she is feeding, bathing and dressing him. In this way the child cottons on to the fact that speech is connected in a rather special way with his world and this is most important for the development of speech and language.

The period from about four to nine months is a vital one for speech development because it is then that the baby begins to 'babble'. This is the time when he lies in his cot or his pram, on waking up or before going to sleep, and makes streams of sound of one sort and another, repeating syllables over and over again, stringing them together and in fact 'playing at talking'. You have only to eavesdrop for a few moments when this is going on to realize that the baby is having fun; he is getting pleasure simply from uttering sounds, without any reference to the world around him. The importance of this babbling activity for speech is partly due to the fact that the child is busy exploring the possibilities of his sound producing apparatus, learning just what can be done with his larynx, his tongue, his soft palate and his lips and practising the actions through continual repetition. In a way it is a bit like the early stages of learning to play the piano: a child will spend hours learning to play five-finger exercises and scales so that later on he may be able to play a Chopin study or a Beethoven sonata. This music may well contain snatches of those same exercises or scales, but the real importance of them is that they lay the foundations of a technique, that is to say habits of movement, which will adapt itself to whatever demands may be made upon it.

The babbling stage is in some ways one of the more mysterious parts of learning to talk because the sounds a baby makes are not closely related to the language spoken around him. English babies in babbling do not confine themselves to sounds that are needed for English, nor do Japanese babies stick to Japanese sounds. They all do a great deal of very general practice which stands them in good stead later on when they do learn the sounds of their mother tongue. The most vital aspect of this practice for speech is that it involves the linking up in the brain of the circuits which produce speech movements and those which control it, the auditory and kinaesthetic feedbacks. The baby is learning that if he makes his larynx work and at the same time keeps on bringing his lips rhythmically together he will produce the very pleasing sound of 'ba–ba–ba–ba'; he learns the converse too, that if he wants to hear 'ba–ba–ba–ba' he can do so any time by making his larynx work and repeatedly bringing his lips together. The child early becomes very sophisticated about this for you can often catch a baby doing such a sequence in a whisper, which means that he has separated out the effect of the lip movement from the larynx action.

Babbling is an essential stage in speech development then because the child is exploring the possibilities of the talking-box that nature has provided him with, is practising a repertoire of movements, many of which he will need later on and, most important of all, is linking in his brain the circuits concerned with muscle action and feedback control. One of the facts about babbling that is often overlooked is that the baby is certainly not imitating the sounds produced by adult speakers. Listen to a baby babbling for a few minutes and you will be convinced that you would be unable to give a very good imitation of him, so it is not very likely that he is imitating you. As a matter of fact a number of the sounds that he makes will find no place in the English sound system when he comes to learn it. Another indication is that when the baby is truly in the babbling stage, he will not imitate the sounds you produce even if you try specifically to make him do so by hanging over him and repeating the same thing over and over again. If anything happens at all in this situation, it will be that the sound of your voice sets the baby babbling with his own repertoire of sounds, he goes into his own routine.

To speak of the stage a child has reached is only to give a hint as to the general character of the activity he will be most engaged in. Stages in speech development, like those in every other type of learning, merge into each other and cannot be marked off by dates and times. The point at which the child's babbling is frequently triggered off by the sound of an adult voice is however a fairly definite one because it shows that the time is rapidly approaching when the child will begin to get involved with speech as a vehicle for language. Up to this point the baby's activity has had no real connection with language and certainly none with any specific language system. The essence of language lies in its connection with the world outside the speaker and the reference which it makes to that world. The baby's babbling takes place in a private world and no sound or syllable is coupled to some particular aspect of the outside world, so that language, with all the social context it implies, has not yet come into the picture.

Before we begin to explore the stages by which it does so, we may well ask the question why a child should learn to talk at all. The forces which come to bear on the child and persuade him to talk are indeed the social ones which constitute the *raison d'être* of language. They are neatly illustrated by an old story about some parents whose first child turned out to be a rather talkative girl, who was followed at an interval of about two years by a boy. To the dismay of the parents the boy never uttered a word in his first years. The parents did everything they could to find out why this was; the child was obviously bright enough and they were assured that he was not deaf or anything like that. The case was a mystery. Slowly the time passed as the anxious parents saw with growing dismay the passing of his second, third and even fourth birthday with never a word on Peter's part. One morning when the whole family was seated at breakfast, he electrified the rest of them by saying loudly and clearly 'There's no sugar on my cornflakes'. You can imagine the mixture of delight and consternation with which his mother stammered 'But P-P-Peter, why have you never spoken before?' to which Peter replied, rather huffily, 'Well, everything has been all right up till now!'. This sums up very nicely the basic reason why a child learns to talk. It soon becomes apparent to him that the strings of noises which issue from the mouths of adults who inhabit his small world are in some strange way a powerful force which influences what happens in that world and that in fact there is precious little that can happen without the agency of this magical activity. Food and drink appear and they disappear, clothes are put on and they are taken off, delightful things happen and hideous things happen, all preceded by, accompanied by and usually followed by talk, talk, talk. It is little wonder that the baby feels some urge to qualify himself for admission to this powerful club. When it turns out that learning to do it is rather fun anyway, it is not surprising that the overwhelming majority of human beings succeed in converting themselves into *homo loquens* in the space of about five years.

When the baby's babbling is triggered by the sound of the mother's voice this is a sign that speech sounds coming from outside are beginning to have a specific effect on the child and this means in turn that he is getting ready to learn the language system. It serves to illustrate also one of the unvarying principles of speech and language acquisition, namely that everything is learned through the reception of speech before there is any attempt at speech production. This fact is rather hard to digest because all of us, parents, grandparents and everyone else, are naturally hypnotized by what the small child manages to say at any stage and we cannot get over the belief that this is the real indication of his grasp of speech. But anything that the child utters has been recognized long before he makes any attempt to bring it out himself and his mastery of the language system is measured by the differences that he can recognize and distinguish rather than by what he can perform himself. Naturally he will in time learn to produce the things he can recognize but there is a time lag between recognition and production. This principle runs through all stages and all aspects of language learning, whether it be of our mother tongue or of a foreign language. It has already been noted, for example, that when as adults we add a new word to our vocabulary, it comes into the passive vocabulary first; we learn to recognize it and then we may later use it ourselves in conversation.

The system of any language is a vastly complicated affair, as we have seen, with its various levels, its large memory stores, its statistics, its laws and its routines and one may well wonder where on earth a child can make a start in learning his native language. One has to realize that acquiring one's first or native language is essentially a different matter from learning a foreign language at a later age; it hinges on learning the trick of what language is. It is tempting to think of the child's brain as being ready furnished with an enormous card index or a mammoth set of pigeonholes or file boxes waiting for him to learn the right things to put into each of them. But no language can possibly work like that because the pigeonholes are themselves the language system and there cannot be empty ones; the child has to build the framework as he goes along, starting with a couple of pigeonholes and adding new ones as he needs them, often by dividing an existing one and putting a partition down the middle. When we learn a foreign language, we already know what a language is, even though the knowledge is not very explicit, and so we know that the new language we are going to learn has a certain framework and that we shall have to learn a collection of words, sounds, grammatical and syntactic units and so on. In the brain of the child learning his mother tongue the language system evolves and it is the social pressures from outside that ensure that it evolves in such a way that he can make sense of what people say to him and they can make sense of what he says to them.

Basically there are two parts to the trick of language: the first part is simply that noises stand for things and the second part is that different noises stand for different things. The noises we generally think of as words, so this means that when things are different there will be different words for them. We have already seen, however, that differences between words are maintained by the operation of the phoneme system, so it is clear that evolving some kind of phoneme system will be among the first steps in learning the trick of language. We speak of a baby's first word and about a small child's learning new words, and rightly so because it is the words that stand for things, but in the early stages these words are essentially the medium through which the phoneme system evolves.

In considering how this comes about we have to bear in mind all the time the two guiding principles of language acquisition, that recognition comes before production and that systems are built up a step at a time. The first language noise a baby recognizes in most cases is the name for the person who is the source of all good things, /mama/, and he does so because this string of sounds is repeatedly uttered in situations where she is obviously involved. The signs that the baby recognizes the word are usually missed because they are so mixed up with the indications that he recognizes the person herself, by turning his head, by smiling and so on, and this is inevitable since most of the time it is mummy herself who is saying her own name. If you watch carefully, however, you can see the word evoking the reaction for some time before the child makes a real attempt to imitate the sound of it himself. At this stage the baby has picked out one morsel of speech and associated it with something quite specific in the world around him and this is the beginning of language.

There is at the same time quite a lot of pressure on the child to produce the word himself; everyone is eagerly awaiting his first word and it is being fed to him frequently in the hope that he will imitate it; in the end he does, much to the satisfaction of all concerned. The first attempts at imitation are distinct from the babbling activity for which the sound of adult speech acts only as a trigger and not as a model for imitation. Of course it is no accident that the name the mother gives herself is a simple syllable repeated because she is influenced by the sort of thing that goes on in babbling, where strings of repeated syllables give the child a great deal of pleasure. Imitating /mama/ or something like it can follow on naturally from babbling and once the link between the word and the person is firmly established by recognition, it is not too long before the child reproduces it.

This first word, recognized and then imitated, contains more than is obvious at first sight, more than the principle that the noise stands for the thing. The sequence is made up of a slightly softer sound followed by a slightly louder one and then the whole thing repeated. This embodies both the idea of the syllable and the idea that order is important, for the name he hears is always /mama/ and never by any chance /amam/. We can scarcely talk about a system being involved as yet because there is no question of different noises standing for different things at this stage, but as soon as the baby recognizes a second word as being attached to a different thing, there is a language system in existence in his brain. The second word is most often /dada/ which becomes associated with the rather strange being who tends to come home at the end of the day and perhaps have a jolly five minutes with the baby at the point when mummy is out on her feet, having coped with the little angel for ten hours at a stretch. In order that the new word shall operate successfully it must be consistently distinguished from /mama/. The form of the word is very similar, the rhythm is the same, the loud parts of the syllables are the same, and the only feature that differentiates them is located in the /m/ and the /d/. Since the baby knows which word is which, his brain must have discovered some way of distinguishing /d/ from /m/, in other words it has fastened on to some acoustic cue which will do the job. Although /mama/ is made up of two syllables, the sound is continuous right through the /m/ and the vowel each time, so that there are two little swells of sound, but in /dada/ the sound is interrupted by a short silence, a kind of hiccough. The child's brain has only to pin its attention to this difference between the continuous and the interrupted sound and it will be able to tell infallibly when it hears /mama/ and when it hears /dada/. The child is now operating a language system, one which has not only two words attached to two things, but also three phonemes: /m/, /d/ and /a/. Now phoneme systems will only work as a whole and these three phonemes make a complete system, a mini-system if you like. There are only three pigeonholes and there is something to place in each of them. As we said earlier, it is not a case of having forty pigeonholes all ready waiting to be used for different phonemes later on; the child must build the framework as he goes along and at present it consists of just three boxes.

Notice also that his brain has found acoustic cues which are only as complicated as the situation demands.

Let us follow our hypothetical baby a little further and imagine that the third word he recognizes consistently is a name for a grandparent, perhaps /nana/. To do this he must be able to distinguish not only /m/ and /d/ but also /m/ and /n/ and of course /d/ and /n/. The difference between the continuous and the interrupted sound will no longer do the whole job because both /m/ and /n/ are continuous, so some other way has to be found to separate these two sounds. It may be hard to believe but there is good sound evidence that even at this early age babies are capable of noticing the differences in second formant transition mentioned in an earlier chapter. When we first hear about this acoustic cue it seems to be an extremely subtle and sophisticated method of distinguishing between sounds, but we have to remember that if we use it as adults it is because we learned to do so as children. There is not much doubt that when the baby recognizes the difference between /mama/ and /nana/ he is relying on the transition cue. In doing so he has expanded his phoneme system by one and there are now four pigeonholes with something to go into each.

The next step might be the addition of a name for the other grandparent, perhaps /baba/ and again the child's brain has a fresh problem. Up till now the interrupted sound always signalled /dada/ but here is a second interrupted sound which must be differentiated because it is attached to a different person. At this point we can see something of the economy of phoneme systems because this small group of two interrupted sounds can be effectively split by the use of the second formant transition cue which already differentiates the two continuous sounds, /m/ and /n/. The brain evolves only the cues that are needed to make the required distinctions and with the system in its present form three cues are enough: the softer–louder cue takes care of the vowel parts of the syllables; the continuous–interrupted cue puts the /m,n/ on one side and the /d,b/ on the other, and then the transition cue separates both /n/ from /m/ and /d/ from /b/. Once more the phoneme system is complete as it stands, with a framework of five pigeonholes for the five phonemes to be distinguished, and it happens that the job can be done with three acoustic cues.

It is important to keep clearly in mind the mechanism by which these developments come about. The first factor is that some person or some thing in the baby's small world takes on a particular interest for him, causing him for the time being to be specially attentive to the word which is associated with it. In order to be sure when this word is said, he has to be able to distinguish it reliably from the other words he already recognizes and his brain sets about the task of finding a cue which is effective. This will quite probably mean that a new phoneme has to be set up, very often by splitting an existing class, as we saw in the case first of the continuous sounds and then of the interrupted ones. So although the child's unconscious purpose is to learn a new word, because of the nature of the language system, he is busy forging for himself an ever expanding phoneme system. We can scarcely follow through step by step the expansion of the system up to the forty-member adult system of English and in any case there is great variation in the way this is done by individual children. The principle, however, is always that which has been illustrated: a phoneme system at every stage complete in itself and determined by the distinctions between words that have to be made. Not every new word recognized calls for a fresh phoneme; it may present existing phonemes in a new order, as is the case for every word learned by an adult, but from time to time a new group of sounds and a new cue become necessary. The child whom we left with the five phoneme system will find the need a little later to notice the hissing sounds which occur in English words; perhaps he gets rather interested in his *shoe*. This hissing sound is a continuous one like /m, n/ but of a very different character so he will pick out the hiss as a fresh kind of sound. But at first all hisses will be the same for him and will form just one class until some new word forces him to split up the hisses, to put a partition in the pigeonhole used for them and to realize that *shoe* and *sock* start off with different hisses, one low-pitched and the other high-pitched. By this kind of process the phoneme framework expands and expands as the child feels the pressure of interest in external things and his brain evolves the acoustic cues needed to make the additional distinctions. By the time the child is about five years old, he will have learned to recognize all the differences involved in the adult system of phonemes, that is in English the forty-odd classes of sound. He cannot yet of course produce in his own speech sounds which adequately embody all these distinctions, but he is now operating with the adult system because he uses it in the reception of speech. Again we have to remember that reception runs ahead of production, that is to say that during the period of language acquisition there is a time lag between the development of recognition and production. One often hears a mother say about her baby at a certain stage 'He understands everything you say to him' and she is implying that he cannot yet say all that he understands; she has noted the time lag between reception and production.

The ability to talk is developing at its own pace all this time, so we will now take a look at what is happening on this side. The baby wants to talk in order to influence events in the world around him and recognition stages are a step to this end. As soon as some progress has been made in speech reception he will try his hand, or his tongue rather, at wielding the magic himself. One might think that with all the practice he put in during the babbling stage this should not give him too much trouble, but in fact it does. The practice was generalized practice which was not linked to a language system and it is an interesting and vital fact that articulations which the baby produced readily in the earlier period cannot simply be called back and pressed into service for the purposes of the phoneme system. Differences in articulation must now be tailored systematically to the demands of the language and this is why prior recognition is so important. The child's aim is to reproduce in his own speech the acoustic cues his brain has evolved for taking in other people's.

In a general sense this is brought about through imitation, mainly of his mother's speech, which is also of course the source of his ability to recognize. In the previous chapter we saw that our own speech reaches us in a unique and private version so that when the child imitates there can never be anything like a perfect match between the sounds he hears from other people and the results of his attempts to imitate. What he can do, however, is to try to make sounds in which he detects the acoustic cues he has already learned. This accounts for the lag between reception and production; it takes time for the continually expanding framework of reception to exert its influence on his articulations. He begins with cues that are effective for the distinctions he needs to make and these, from the viewpoint of the complete adult system, are gross distinctions like that between a continuous and an interrupted sound or, at a later stage, between an interrupted and a hissing sound, without any discrimination among the various hissing sounds. When this type of cue is applied to the child's own speech it gives rise to all the childish pronunciations which parents and indeed all the rest of us find so delightful. For some time he will be content to form syllables with almost any kind of interruption, producing sequences like /pudi tat/ for *pussy cat* or /iku gogi/ for *little doggie*. As time goes on the child will be recognizing a wider and wider range of things and will do his best to reproduce them, getting in whatever cues he can; he will tackle things like /bano/ for *piano*, /dohin/ for *dolphin*, /budlozer/ for *bulldozer*, /cocker bisik/ for *chocolate biscuit* and so on. He is doing his best to embody in his own sounds the cues he uses in recognition but obviously what he produces is not all that easy for his listeners to decode. His best audience from every point of view is his mother and there is always a stage when she acts as his interpreter to the rest of the world; but he will not be satisfied for very long if there is only one person whose actions can be influenced by his speech so there is constant pressure on him to modify his pronunciation in order to make what he says easily understood by a wider circle of adults. He can do this by introducing progressively more of the cues his brain has evolved for speech reception. Some distinctions are more difficult for him to manage than others; he may well be halfway through his fifth year before he can articulate very presentable /th/ sounds or an /r/ sound like that of most of the adults around him. Some groups of consonants will give him trouble for quite a long time. For English children the distinction between the initial sounds of *chain* and *train* is a difficult one to achieve. It will probably not have struck you that they are at all alike but if you say the two words in succession, you will notice that the acoustic effect is remarkably similar, the first being just a little higher pitched than the second. Here again the child will have learned to recognize the distinction long before he can produce it and it is interesting that, even when he can pronounce the two sounds, he finds it hard to know when to use one and when to use the other. You may for instance hear a child at this stage say *treeks* for *cheeks*, *trin* for *chin* and *satrel* for *satchel*. Another confusion that occurs is between /tr/ and /tw/ and this is understandable since for a long time the child has probably been saying /w/ in place of /r/, *wed wabbit* and so on. When he at last succeeds in making the difference, he will still be in doubt when to use each of them and may come out with *trelve* for *twelve*, *trist* for *twist*, or even rather charmingly 'Trinkle, trinkle little star'.

While the child's pronunciation is shaped mainly by the pressure of the phoneme system, it is at the same time the result of imitation, in normal circumstances of his mother's speech. The phoneme system itself is derived from this model which is responsible also for the more detailed quality of the sounds produced, what is often referred to as the 'accent' of the speaker. In English this is very largely a matter of the quality of the vowel sounds, in which the language system allows a good deal more variation than in the consonants. In determining this aspect of a child's speech, the mother's accent is usually paramount even where it differs from that of most of the other adults who surround the child. A child of a Scottish mother, brought up from birth in London, say, is almost certain to speak with a Scottish accent to some degree. The same influence is strong, too, in deciding characteristics of rhythm and intonation, both the grammatical component of intonation and its use in the expression of emotion. Children begin very early to imitate the tunes of the mother's speech but just as the pronunciation of vowels and consonants is shaped by the need to be understood, so the use of tone and rhythm is modified so as to convey what is intended to a whole circle of adult listeners.

By the time a child is about five years old, then, he has built up by a process of expansion a phoneme system which coincides with that of the adult language around him, he has evolved a set of acoustic cues that enable him to recognize all the necessary distinctions when he is listening to speech, he has applied the knowledge of these cues to his own speech so as to make it intelligible, at least with some degree of good will, to those around him, he has learned to recognize and to produce the appropriate rhythm and intonation patterns and his pronunciation has taken on through imitation most of the features that will characterize his accent. Yet all this has been done, as we said earlier, by learning new words; one might almost say that these other things are a by-product, though an absolutely essential by-product, of his adding to his vocabulary. In conformity with the general principle, the additions are to his passive vocabulary first, though in these early stages of language acquisition we can be fairly sure that all words will pass from the passive to the active vocabulary. It will be well to consider at this point just what happens as the new words are learned.

For the small child, words are noises which stand for things or people and when he knows only a handful of words, they can stand for only a few items in his world. One of the interesting things that happens is that the area which one word covers for the child changes as time passes; one can say, if you like, that the meaning of the word expands and contracts. A very clear example of this is the word /dada/. When the baby first learns it, it refers to the one person who appears at somewhat lengthy intervals and is so named by mummy. Some weeks later, however, when the child is at the stage of being taken out in the streets by his mother, the meaning of this word expands to include almost any figure in trousers and perhaps a moustache or beard, no matter where or when he appears. The child will then hail loudly any such figure as 'Dada', not without embarrassment to mummy. The meaning of the word will contract again, however, when another word is added to the vocabulary, the word *man*, which is soon seen to refer to the general class and the word /dada/ reverts to its reference to one person only.

Because the world is so full of a number of things, even for a small child, and because he has to build up his store of words bit by bit, this kind of fluctuation in the area of reference of a word goes on continually. One small boy, for instance, learned the word *ladder*, which he pronounced incidentally /ladler/, when the house opposite to his own was being painted. But in a short space of time /ladler/ meant for him a ladder, anything at all propped against the side of a house, any shape such as the back of a garden seat with parallel members and slats across *and* any man in white overalls. Of course it was only a matter of time before the learning of a few additional words would reduce the reference of the word once again until it meant simply – a ladder. For another small boy, at one period, *rain* meant not only wet stuff that fell but also *a reason for not going out*. In perfectly fine weather at midday, when it was too hot to go into the garden, he would go to the door, hold out his hand and say 'Rain', not as a question but as a statement meaning 'we don't go out'.

This brings up another important aspect of the function of words in the early stages of language development. Just as a word can cover a wide area of reference, so it can also function as the equivalent of an adult sentence. This is particularly the case when the child gets to the stage of putting two words together, an important development which we shall be looking at in a moment. For example, when the child says 'Mummy coat' this may simply mean 'That's mummy's coat' but it may also mean 'Where is mummy's coat?' or again 'Mummy should put her coat on so that we can go out'. Even the single word at an earlier stage will have different functions in different situations. /mama/ may at one time mean 'The name of the person I can see is Mama' but on another occasion it may mean 'The hat I'm pointing to belongs to Mama' or it may be the equivalent of the expression 'Mama do it', which the child will use later on. While his language has no explicit grammar, he will use the words he knows with different functions so that adding to his vocabulary is something rather more than just adding to his stock of words. At the age of eighteen months he may be using no more than about twenty words in this way but even three months later the number may have risen to something like two hundred.

Up to this point whatever the child says is basically an imitation of what he hears, though he is making it serve a rather wider range of functions. At about the age of two a great step forward is taken when the child strings two words together, because when this happens his mini-language now has a grammar. In an earlier chapter it was said that grammar is not to be thought of as the host of complicated rules which we were supposed to learn, not without tears, in our schooldays, rules which we were expected to adhere to when speaking or writing and which we were continually 'breaking'. Real grammar is concerned with what people do when they talk and not with what they *should* do, and it consists of the principles of structure and sequence which apply when any given language is used. As soon as the small child puts two words together in English, he develops a principle, that is effectively a syntax, which controls the order of the words. This is the period when he will use over and over again such expressions as 'Bye-bye Mummy', 'Bye-bye sock', 'Bye-bye boat' and 'All-gone milk', 'All-gone flakes', 'All-gone car', 'All-gone soap' and so on. In all of these the names of different things are combined with a kind of operator word to make what are really sentences in the child language, in which the operator word must come first and then the name. When this principle is established, any new words will appear first in the name class, having of course been learned through recognition. A few very familiar words make up the operators but as time goes on words may pass from the name class into this class. While the child limits his remarks to two-word sequences, he will keep to this basic construction, that is to this syntax.

This stage in language development is extremely interesting because it differs from everything that has gone before. Up to this point the child's sounds and words have been copied from the speech of his mother or of other adults, but here quite suddenly is a development which does not represent a pattern that has been copied. Adults do not spontaneously say things like 'All-gone milk', which do not form part of their language. It is true that mothers may sometimes be concerned about 'teaching the child baby-talk' or they may be reproached by others for doing so. But the boot is entirely on the other foot and it is the baby who teaches mummy baby-talk. When adults use such expressions, they are doing so in imitation of the baby who is now creating his own language and not simply repeating what he hears. This step forward in the use of language represents very much a development in thinking because it means that the child is already grasping the principle which lies behind the use of verbs as well as nouns. From this point onwards, new words learned will eventually fall into different classes because of the different ways in which they will function in the language.

Combinations of an operator word and a name will meet the child's needs for some time but before very long he will extend his technique to include strings of three or four words. Many of his remarks may begin to sound like adult sentences but he will still use only words essential to his meaning and in most cases will keep to his own kind of syntax, producing sequences like 'Where you are?' and 'Mummy biscuits got?' which show clearly that he is evolving for himself the technique of making up sentences and is not just copying strings of words heard from adults.

The ensuing period in the child's life sees what is actually the most spectacular achievement that the child makes in any direction. In the space of about two short years the majority of children progress from remarks like 'Bye-bye sock' to quite complicated sentences on the adult model, things like 'Mummy, I don't think this tractor's as strong as the one Daddy bought me last week'. We take all this as a matter of course and do not realize how miraculous the process is. The child gets hours and hours of practice, virtually all his waking moments, since he is continually surrounded by adult speech. What he does is to infer from the thousands of examples he hears the principles of grammar and syntax which are operating in his native language and it is this that constitutes the most remarkable part of his achievement. With nearly every child there comes a point where language itself becomes intensely interesting and this serves to make his practice still more concentrated. Adults seldom realize that the child who is at the 'Why?' 'What's that?' stage is expressing his curiosity about words rather than

Age 0–2 months
Discomfort sounds

Age 2–4 months
Add pleasure sounds

Age 4–9 months
Babbling

Age 9–18 months
Building phoneme system

Age 18 months–$2\frac{1}{2}$ years
Two-word phrases

Age $2\frac{1}{2}$–4 years
Learn grammar, expand vocabulary
Complete phoneme system

Age 4–6 years
Adult grammar and syntax

The average child does not exist. If he did, he would probably reach the successive stages of speech and language development within the periods suggested in this table.

things. A mother who has had to reply to the question 'What's that?' by saying 'A bicycle' a hundred times over may be forgiven for thinking her son is passionately interested in bicycles, but the truth is rather that he is learning the word *bicycle* and has to have it repeated many times to make sure he has got it. The same thing holds good with regard to the form of sentences and phrases. The question 'Why?' is an excellent way of hitting the jackpot of variations on a construction. We may imagine the child wants to know why, whereas he is much more keen to check that in reply you can say 'Because it is not so-and-so' or 'Because it is too so-and-so' or 'Because I haven't so-and-so' and even if he turns up a few 'don't knows', it has been well worth while from his point of view.

Systematic observation of children's speech during this period of language development produces convincing evidence that the child's brain is formulating the principles of the grammar for itself. Just from hearing what adults say the English child will infer, for example, that if something took place in the past you put *-ed* on to the end of words in one particular class, that if you have more than one of a thing, you add *-s* to another class of words, that if some quality is more in one case than in another, you put *-er* on to the word which refers to this quality, and so on. Within a short time the child's brain is stocked with formulations of this kind which he then applies in his own speech. He will apply them quite generally and most of the time this will produce acceptable remarks but sometimes the words which he forms in this way by analogy will not correspond to the usage of the adult language. When he has discovered how to make verbs refer to the past by ending them in *-ed*, he will use forms like *bringed, standed* and *teached* and similarly he will make plurals such as *mouses* and *scissorses* and comparative forms like *gooder* and *badder*. People are inclined to say that this is because he has not yet learned English grammar, but the reverse is the truth: he does it because he *has* learned English grammar, or rather has inferred its laws for himself since it is clear that he has not heard these forms used by adult speakers.

Examples of many different kinds of formation by analogy

can be culled from children's speech, some affecting sentence construction and word formation as can be seen in the two following examples, both of which display a rather charming inventiveness. The first occurred in the speech of a small boy who was heard to exclaim 'You'd never do that, never'd you?', thereby showing an essential grasp of a complicated routine for converting a statement with an auxiliary verb into a question. The second concerns a father who, hearing something of a fracas breaking out in another room between an older and a younger daughter, called out loudly 'Deborah, tell Elizabeth not to argue!'. What was his surprise, and since he was a linguist his delight too, to hear a childish voice say in authoritative tones 'Elizabeth, don't arg me'. This is an interesting illustration of the child's ability to get the morpheme string appropriately arranged even when not too sure of the content of the words. In the natural course of events, as the child hears more and more adult speech, words like *standed, teached, mouses, gooder* and so on give way to the adult forms, sometimes with explicit help from the parents, and ultimately the child's speech conforms in usage with that of the adults among whom he lives.

The development of grammar and syntax, like that of the phoneme system, takes place through the learning of new words. All of them go first into the passive vocabulary but in the early stages the child needs above all words to use, so that they pass fairly rapidly into his active vocabulary. It often happens that towards the middle of the second year the child concentrates on enlarging his passive vocabulary, which grows very quickly, and comparatively few new words appear in his own speech. During this time a child will usually refuse to repeat a word which he is just learning to recognize; there has to be some time lag before he will even say it aloud, let alone use it spontaneously in his own speech. In the ensuing months there is quite likely to be a marked increase in the number of words he transfers to his active vocabulary.

The words which are entered in our brain dictionary fall into a number of different word classes and three of these, the prepositions, conjunctions and pronouns, have a fixed number of items. During the period of language acquisition we learn the complete list of entries in these classes just as we learn the entire list of bound morphemes and all this material taken together determines the form of what we say as distinct from its content. It is part of the economy of language that the form is regulated by choosing from a finite and restricted number of different elements, while the content is determined by choice from an infinitely greater range of possibilities. Language acquisition would scarcely be a practical proposition were it not for this arrangement; when we learn our mother tongue, we are able to acquire the complete stock of information demanded by the form of a spoken message during the learning period and as our experience and our mental powers increase, we employ these forms to express an ever greater variety of content. Consequently the words which we add to our cortical dictionary throughout life fall into the remaining word classes, nouns, verbs, adjectives and adverbs. Of these the nouns are the most numerous class, with verbs next, with adjectives some way behind and adverbs fewer still. These proportions are reflected in the child's language development. He begins by amassing a comparatively large stock of nouns and only one or two verbs; then about the age of two he will generally enlarge his stock of verbs rather rapidly, though the number will never equal that of the nouns. At this stage he will know a few adjectives, perhaps an adverb or two and one or two interrogative words such as *what* and *where*. It is obvious that mental development and language development go hand in hand and interact very much with each other. The child's grasp of the relations of things in the outside world and his ability to carry out mental operations do a great deal to influence the order in which some word classes grow. A child does not find it easy even to understand the meaning of prepositions, for example, and he therefore does not use them in an early stage of his language learning. At the age of about two he may learn a few, such as *to, in* and *on,* but it will be a long time before he can use words like *under, behind* and *before*. In a similar way he will use the word *and* quite early, but he will be at the stage of putting together complex sentences before he can handle *but, if* and *though*. Up to the age of two or more, a child refers to himself by name and in the third person and therefore pronouns do not appear in his speech until he begins to refer to himself as *me* or *I*, other pronouns coming into his vocabulary later still.

Individual children naturally develop in their own way and at their own pace with respect to speech and language as they do with everything else and the average child remains a figment of the statistical imagination. We may say, as a rough guide to the rate at which vocabulary grows, however, that at two years of age a child may be using about 200 different words; at three this will have risen to about 1000, and at four to something like 2000. You may recall that the estimate of adult active vocabulary was 4000–5000 words and it may seem strange that the rest of one's life leads to no more than a two-to-one increase. The point is, however, that the 2000 words the child commands comprise the form words, the prepositions, conjunctions and pronouns, and all the commonest nouns and verbs, without which we should not be able to say anything at all, so the twofold increase leaves a considerable margin for the less common words, the technical and specialist vocabularies which characterize the speech of individual adult speakers.

The task of learning our mother tongue, then, is one which we accomplish essentially in the first five years of life. We evolve for ourselves the phoneme system, the acoustic cues for distinguishing sounds, the grammar and the syntax, and we lay the foundations of our personal dictionary. All this is derived from the sound of adult speech by which we are continually surrounded and we copy, mainly from our mothers, our pronunciation, intonation and rhythm. There may be some modifications in the last three in the course of our subsequent experience, but it is extremely difficult to make radical changes in our speech habits, as we all learn when we attempt to acquire a foreign language. Because we devote such an enormous amount of practice to the task, we are able to complete it painlessly and to forget it thereafter but this does not detract from the magnitude of the achievement. Only a few short years separate the bawling baby from the fully paid up member of the club of *homo loquens*. A well-known psychologist once remarked after four full days of discussion of the subject that he still favoured the 'miracle theory' of language acquisition and the more one discovers about speech, the more one is inclined to agree with him.

9

Are you left-brained or right-brained?

In the brain are male and female faculties: here is marriage, here is fruit.
Ralph Waldo Emerson

There are two modes of knowledge, through argument and experience.
Roger Bacon

So much has been said about the part played by the brain in all matters connected with speech that it is high time we directed our attention to one of the most intriguing aspects of brain functioning. It has been known for many centuries, indeed the fact was recognized by Hippocrates, that the brain is divided into two halves both from the anatomical and the functional point of view. The two parts, the cerebral hemispheres, are placed side by side within the skull with a vertical division between them and in appearance they are not unlike what one sees inside the shell of a walnut, except that they are covered with a grey matter which we are all so proud of possessing. The two hemispheres are connected together by means of what we might think of as a many stranded telephone cable, the *corpus callosum*, along which messages constantly pass from one hemisphere to another. Both hemispheres are on duty twenty-four hours a day just keeping us alive, and for this they are both equally important. The interesting feature of their arrangement, from our point of view, is that each hemisphere receives information from and controls movement in the opposite side of the body, so that when you do something with your right hand, it is the left hemisphere that is in charge and when you do it with your left hand, the right hemisphere is controlling the action. As regards information reaching the brain from the outside world, the right ear does send some of its acoustic information to the right brain, but most of it is transmitted directly to the left hemisphere, and the opposite is the case for the left ear. The set-up for vision is a bit more complicated than this; if you look straight ahead of you, then everything which is in the left half of the visual field for both eyes transmits information to the right hemisphere and what is in the right half of the field goes to the left brain. This intricate scheme for supplying the brain with information from the two ears and eyes is important, among other things, as the basis of our ability to locate sights and sounds in space and to judge distances.

Human bodies are never completely symmetrical, either in their structure or their functioning and it is especially true of the hands that one is more 'handy' than the other. For a considerable majority of people it is the right hand that has more facility for doing actions calling for a marked degree of control. The bias towards right-handedness is in fact so strong that we use the words 'dexterous' and 'adroit' to mean clever and skilful, while someone who is awkward is 'gauche' and unfavourable actions are 'sinister'. Even the expression 'southpaw' seems mildly derogatory; certainly one never hears anyone referred to as a 'northpaw'. The right hand is under the control of the left brain and consequently this hemisphere is very much concerned in those of our activities which require a degree of skill. An enormous number of things we do call for the use of both hands so that control is shared for much of the time, but for most of us there is little doubt that one hand performs tasks more easily and readily than the other, so that we may justifiably regard it as the dominant hand. In this case we must also regard one of the hemispheres as being *dominant* and it is generally true that in right-handed people the left hemisphere is the dominant half of the brain.

The principal reason for describing the left brain as dominant in right-handed people is, however, not so much its control of the more skilful hand as the fact that it is in the left hemisphere that the control of speech develops. This means not only the control of movements but also the memory stores and all the processing circuits concerned with speech and language. The dominant hemisphere is therefore dominant for speech. It has been known for well over a century that one half of the brain is specialized for speech, the evidence having been gathered from the study of cases in which damage to the brain gave rise to difficulties with speech and language or to the total loss of language capacity. There will be more to say on this subject in the following chapter, but briefly it was consistently found that in right-handed patients it was damage to the left brain that affected speech, the difficulty being accompanied by some degree of paralysis on the right side of the body; brain damage on the right side generally failed to produce any interference with speech, though it led to paralysis on the left side of the body. In more recent times a variety of observations carried out on patients who were undergoing brain surgery has amply confirmed the view that one hemisphere usually specializes in all the complex operations connected with speech and language, and that this hemisphere is the one which controls the master hand.

The last statement does call for some qualification, however, because a word needs to be said about left-handers. As far as present evidence goes, people who are congenitally right-handed develop speech and language centres in the left hemisphere, but left-handed people form a group which is by no means as homogeneous. For one thing, the right-handed bias of our society still causes some left-handers to be trained to write with the right hand and to develop a habit of doing other things with the right hand that they would not spontaneously do. Many of them become suppressed left-handers and many others are what we call ambidexterous. In these days of almost universal indignation, it is rather surprising that there is no movement for the liberation of left-handers, perhaps with an agitation for replacing the word *ambidexterous* by the word *ambisinistral*. There is a growing body of evidence to suggest that left-handed people fall into one of at least three classes. In some of them the brain dominance for speech and language is reversed, with the control of the master hand and the control of speech in the right brain. Others have the speech and language circuits in the left hemisphere, although the master hand is controlled by the opposite side of the brain, and a third group have what is called 'mixed dominance', that is to say that circuits concerned with speech develop on both sides of the brain, though it is not clear whether this arrangement constitutes a duplication or a division of language control. It is possible that many of those children who have great difficulty in learning to read belong to this third group.

Finding out what the brain is doing is no easy task in any circumstances. Most of what we know about the subject is arrived at simply by inferring from the effects of brain activity, that is from the actions of the person involved. There is no way in which we can take a picture of the brain, and if there were, it would not help us very much because it would be somewhat like taking an X-ray picture of a television set that was not switched on. We judge the television set by the picture and the sound which it sends out and we have to do the same with the brain. A start has been made on the use of more direct observations of brain activity through the electro-encephalograph, the machine that registers brain waves, and a great deal is being learned by this method, as we shall see later on, but still people's behaviour is our major source of information. In many ways the human brain remains what scientists call a 'black box' and we learn most about it by comparing what goes into it with what comes out.

Cases of brain damage have in the past provided practically all that was known about brain activity in relation to speech and language. In any context we have to be rather cautious in generalizing from a pathological condition to normal working, but the knowledge gained in this way about speech has been invaluable. Quite recently it has been added to dramatically by the study of a particular condition which is so relevant to the subject of brain dominance that it will be worth while to spend a little time on it. There are some patients who suffer from epileptic seizures of such severity and so continuously that any sort of ordinary life is impossible for them and they suffer grave physical injury very often at the onset of the seizures. It has been discovered that one factor which contributes to the severity of the attacks is the transmission of nerve messages back and forth between the two brain hemispheres, the setting up of a kind of reverberance. You will remember that the path for transmission between the halves of the brain is the *corpus callosum*. A surgical technique has been developed for cutting this connection in patients of the kind just described with a resulting reduction in both the number and the severity of the seizures. The immediately surprising thing about these 'split-brain' patients, apart from the very desirable improvement in their general well-being, is that the separation of the two halves of the brain does not produce any noticeable abnormalities in their ordinary behaviour. It may not be at once obvious why one should expect such abnormalities, but when we remember that all the capacity for speech and language is on one side of the brain, we can see that cutting the interconnection means depriving the other side of any access to this vital means of communication with the outside world. We have two eyes and two ears, we have nerve connections from our limbs and our organs to both halves of the brain and all these are intact in the split-brain patient; this is the reason why in the circumstances of everyday life their behaviour is not in any way extraordinary. When they do certain kinds of test in a laboratory, however, it becomes clear just what the effect of cutting the connection is.

One of the things which is possible in laboratory tests is to ensure that sensory information is delivered to one side of the brain only, something which does not usually happen in ordinary life. When this is done in the case of the split-brain patient, it is demonstrated conclusively that the right side of the brain (and we are referring to right-handed patients) simply does not know how to talk. If something is made visible to the patient only in the right half of the field for each eye, the visual information is relayed to the left hemisphere only and the patient can answer questions and converse about what he has seen. But if the experiment is repeated with the left half of each visual field, so that information reaches the right brain only, then the patient is quite unable to say anything about what he has seen, because the talking half of the brain has not seen it and will be quite mystified as to the reason for the questions. Evidently there is no way in which the right side of the brain can tell the left side what it has experienced. One incident which is related about a split-brain woman patient brings this home in a graphic way. She was being tested with a series of pictures which were presented to her right brain only. Questions which were put to her involved her left brain, of course, and she was as usual unable to comment on what she saw. During the experiment a picture of a somewhat erotic nature was inserted in the series of ordinary objects, whereupon the patient went very red in the face and appeared very embarrassed but still could not verbalize about the cause of her embarrassment. When the experience was repeated, she continued to be incapable of saying anything about the picture but evidently the general sensation of embarrassment conveyed itself to the left hemisphere and she managed to say eventually 'Oh doctor, you sure have a funny machine!'. The left brain did not even in the end know what had been seen and was only able to express the sensation.

In other experiments with split-brain patients information conveyed by touch has been transmitted to one half of the brain only. If a cut-out shape in wood or plastic, let us say a circle, a square or a triangle, is placed in the right hand of the patient without his being able to see the shape, the sense of touch will tell his left brain what the shape is and, because the left brain can speak, he will be able to answer correctly every time when asked which of the three shapes he has been given. The left hand, however, will send the information to the right brain; because the communication line is cut, the right hemisphere is unable to send the news across to the left brain which will answer at random when asked which shape is held in the hand. This is exactly what happened when the experiment was tried with split-brain patients; the right hand gave a hundred per cent correct answers but the left hand produced answers which were about one-third circle, one-third square and one-third triangle, regardless of how often each shape was used. The later stages of the experiment, however, gave rise to a most astonishing result, for it was found that eventually even with the left hand patients began to score quite a high proportion of correct answers and this was at first inexplicable. It was then noticed that when, say, a circle was placed in the left hand, the patient would begin to look round the room and pick out some circular object, perhaps a clock, and would then move his head in a circle. The left hemisphere, given the clue by the movement, would then give the right answer 'Circle' and it was by the use of this technique that patients succeeded in scoring a high number of correct responses. This is a truly wonderful illustration of the extreme adaptability of the human brain. The right hemisphere, deprived of a direct line of communication with the left, evolved the device of going out into the external world and finding there some stimulus which could send the necessary information in to the left hemisphere.

The behaviour of split-brain patients has now been very extensively and intensively studied and as a result we know that each hemisphere *can* continue its life independently of the other; each one by itself can be aware of things, can learn and can remember things. Evidently the biblical injunction 'Let not the right hand know what the left hand doeth' would be unnecessary were it not for the connection which links the two halves of the normal brain; in the split-brain patient it is the permanent state of affairs. Moreover, each half of the brain is specialized for rather different activities or, more precisely, is designed to cope with what comes into the system in a different way. The left brain deals with speaking and listening, with reading and writing. Because language in all its forms plays such a dominant part in our lives this constitutes the principal characteristic of this half of the brain, but it exemplifies in fact a more general feature, the tendency to deal with things in sequence. All that has been said about speech and language so far serves to underline that the whole process consists in stringing elements together, whatever the level of operation involved. The fact that B follows A, or that x precedes y and z is vital information with regard to a spoken or a written message. The sequences are not only temporal but also logical in the sense that B follows from A, so the left brain is the specialist in logical and sequential analysis.

What then is the speciality of the right brain? Basically it is that, where the left brain prefers to deal with everything in sequence, the right brain deals with a whole pattern at one time; its natural method of working is what is often referred to as *gestalt* operation. For this reason any activity that involves spatial relations, where a number of factors have to be appreciated simultaneously, is likely to be the province of the right brain. Obviously among our daily occupations some will require mainly work from the left hemisphere while others need right hemisphere work, but it must be stressed again that the difference between the two halves of the brain is essentially in their way of going about things. This can be illustrated by an extreme example taken from experiments with split-brain patients. In the visual experiments one of the patterns conveyed to the right and the left brain on different occasions was a line drawing of a cube, which the patient was asked to reproduce. This is typically the kind of material the right brain is designed to deal with and one patient, when it was presented to his right brain, drew a perfectly presentable cube. When it was presented to his left brain, however, what he did was to draw a series of eight corners one under the other; the analysing mechanism of his left brain had simply gone round the figure and registered one angle of the figure after another. This demonstrates very nicely that when the same information is sent to the two hemispheres, each will deal with it in its own way.

Fortunately our ideas about the specialization of the two hemispheres are no longer solely dependent upon the study of pathological cases and the effects of surgical intervention. In a wide range of recent work with the electro-encephalograph (the EEG or brain-wave machine) a great deal has been learned about brain activity in normal people. One of the features of brain-waves that is most widely known is the alpha rhythm or alpha wave. This is a type of brain-wave which is most obvious in the records when the brain is resting so that if it is measured in suitable conditions, it can be used as a negative sign of brain activity. Suppose now that we register brain-waves while a normal person is engaged in doing something which is likely to call for predominantly left-brain activity, we should expect that the right brain would be more or less resting and would therefore give out a comparatively high level of alpha wave. If the task is changed so that right hemisphere work is called for, we should expect the situation to be reversed and a higher level of alpha to be shown by the left hemisphere. This technique has now been applied to a variety of tasks and the results amply confirm the notions arrived at through observation of split-brain patients. While writing out a passage from memory or copying a text or mentally composing a letter, normal right-handed subjects gave a preponderance of alpha from the right side of the head; for other tasks such as drawing something seen in a mirror or constructing with geometrical blocks a pattern illustrated in a two-dimensional drawing, the position was reversed and the higher level of alpha was registered by the left side of the head. There is little doubt therefore that the ordinary person does tend to use each half of his brain for the jobs which suit it; in the case of speech and language he has no choice about this, usually, since only one of the hemispheres has the necessary capacity. We are very far from knowing all there is to know about this specialization but one can say broadly that the left brain (in right-handed people) deals with all matters involving speech and language, with mathematics, with logical and sequential analysis; it is poor at dealing with spatial relations and at taking a *gestalt* view of things. The right brain has only a few words at its disposal and may be capable of arithmetical addition up to a limit of about ten, but it can deal successfully with problems depending on spatial relations, can take a holistic view of things and, incidentally, deals with musical patterns. The last is simply a statement of observed fact which is not entirely easy to fit in with other features since it would seem that much of music depends for its effect upon sequence. It is very likely that not all aspects of music are dealt with in the same way and that musical activity may require a contribution from both halves of the brain.

Our daily life forces us to use both hemispheres all the time. There is no question of switching one of them off completely and going from one job to another does no more than shift the balance from time to time. It is also true that as individuals we tend to have our favourite mode of operation, some of us habitually relying more on a sequential, logical, analytical approach to things while others more readily take a view of the whole and see things in spatial terms rather than temporal. It is possible to show up such preferences also by laboratory tests. For example, a pack of cards is used each of which bears both a drawing and a word, and people are asked to sort the cards very rapidly, using any method they like. The left-brained people will be found to have sorted them predominantly on the basis of the words, whereas the right-brained individuals will have done so on the basis of the drawings.

The question as to what makes each of us on balance a right-brained or a left-brained person is one which we have as yet no basis for beginning to answer, any more than we can answer the further question, which resolves itself into one of the 'chicken-and-egg' variety, as to whether left-brained people gravitate to left-brained occupations or whether left-brained jobs produce left-brained people. One can reasonably guess however that those who work as administrators, lawyers, mathematicians, computer programmers, scientists and in a large proportion of academic pursuits of all kinds, either have or have developed a preference for left-brain working, while architects, painters, sculptors, designers, decorators and the majority of people who make things are probably predominantly right-brained. It may well be that the fellow who is said to be a square peg in a round hole may not infrequently be a right-brained individual in a left-brained job or vice versa. It seems probable at all events that one way to achieve *mens* really *sana* may be to try and ensure that both right and left brain get fairly frequent outings, not to say gallops. The peculiarly English habit of cultivating hobbies very assiduously appears on this basis highly justifiable. The civil servant or lawyer who spends all his spare time playing string quartets and the cabinet maker who has a passion for archaeology may both have adopted the principle without knowing it.

Whenever we are talking or listening, reading or writing, we can be sure that we are putting the left brain to work (if we are right-handed!). The human brain is a marvellously designed piece of apparatus and we are not likely to wear it out by any of these activities. What is more important perhaps is to reflect from time to time that, by changing our activity and ceasing to do any of these things, we may be giving the chance for a little exercise to the other half of our cerebral world and this may be all to the good.

10

When speech goes wrong

> Speech is the birthright of every child.
> Deafness stops up the fountain head of knowledge and turns life into a desert. For without language intellectual life is impossible.
> How I should like to speak like other people! I should be willing to work night and day if it could only be accomplished.
>
> Helen Keller

In the course of the present century speech and all the matters relating to it have become the technical concern of a great many people. Because of what the popular journalist might call the 'communication explosion', engineers in particular have had to ask themselves many questions and to develop new points of view about speech. One of the prejudices which engineers and physicists find it hard to overcome leads them to view speech as an 'inefficient' way of going about things. They compute efficiency in terms of energy expended and work done and therefore regard the redundancy of speech as a symptom of inefficiency. Seen in broader perspective, however, speech proves to be a quite incredibly efficient system because it ensures virtually error-free communication in the face of extreme variability in the signals and sometimes of high levels of distortion and noise. It is the very redundancy of speech that makes this possible and allows us to talk to each other in conditions which would otherwise rule out communication altogether. To take one example that has already been mentioned, the telephone engineer who provides us with a system transmitting just over one-third of the acoustic information in speech is relying very heavily on this feature. If speech were 'efficient' in the engineering sense, then telephones would have to be infinitely more expensive and much more vulnerable devices.

Fortunately speech is extremely resistant to most of the things that may go wrong with it. The speaker can make gross mistakes and the listener corrects them, even if the speaker himself does not; the listener makes mistakes and the context of the message corrects them; the signal becomes very distorted or the channel very noisy, usually both, and we continue our conversation by drawing more and more on our powers of guessing. The lengths to which this can go become fairly obvious when, through the medium of television transmissions, we eavesdrop on the exchanges between astronauts and ground control. Communication by speech breaks down only when there is simply not enough information passing to make the reconstruction of the message possible, because the speech is too faint or the noise and distortion exceed the tolerable limits. Most of the short-term troubles in speech communication therefore are taken care of by the very nature of speech and language.

There are on the other hand some interferences with speech which make communication difficult or impossible and these lie in the speaker or the listener, the human terminals of the communication chain. Certain of them affect the acquiring of speech and language by the child while others make speech difficult or impossible later in life. Before we begin to look at these speech troubles in detail, it will be well to make one general point that has not so far been mentioned. Continual insistence upon the role of the brain in speech may have led readers to associate the ability to speak with a high level of intelligence. It is important to recognize that in fact speech represents a relatively low level of brain activity. Acquiring speech is a truly remarkable feat but it is one that is accessible to practically every human being. It marks a rung on the evolutionary ladder but it does not differentiate among the members of our own species. One has only to make a rapid mental review of the people one is acquainted with to see that this must be the case; the most intelligent person you know talks, but so does the least intelligent and, extending the range much further, it is only the most extreme degree of mental subnormality that prevents a child from acquiring at least the ability to take in speech. In general we do not concern ourselves with the mere mechanics of talking but with the content of what is said and this naturally does indicate differences in mental capacity. As a result we tend to confuse the two things and to overrate the sheer ability to speak. Complex though the mechanism is, and we have devoted many pages to its complexities, the activity is largely automatic and is carried on at a brain level where we need pay it very little attention. When people tackle a foreign language, for instance, they usually make the mistake of doing so at much too high a level and do not appreciate that it is practice in actually saying things and in actually listening to them that really counts, just as it counted in the acquisition of their mother tongue. Very rarely even today are students told that the new language means learning a new phoneme system and yet this is a basic and indispensable part of what they are trying to acquire. Whatever may go wrong with speech, then, either in its practice or its acquisition, it is extremely unlikely to be very much connected with intelligence. After all, if geniuses alone could talk the world would be a delightfully silent place.

In considering some of the factors which may interfere with the learning of speech, let us begin with the most obvious. All the developments that were described in an earlier chapter, building up the phoneme system, controlling speech movements, learning grammar and syntax, adding to the vocabulary, are absolutely dependent on a continual flow of speech sounds coming into the ears and reaching the brain. Any condition which interferes with this will certainly be an obstacle to speech development. A child born with seriously impaired hearing presents a problem from this point of view. Such births are due to a variety of causes, some of them well-known but others as yet quite undetermined. The principal known causes are inherited conditions, infections suffered by the mother during pregnancy and injuries or abnormalities at birth. The dangers of infection during pregnancy, particularly from German measles for example, are widely recognized nowadays and appropriate steps are taken to reduce the risk of severe deafness and other congenital defects from this cause.

In addition to children born with impaired hearing, there are a number whose hearing is damaged by infections such as meningitis very early in life.

A severe loss of hearing, from whatever cause, will interfere with the natural and spontaneous development of the capacity to speak and to take in speech, for it will mean that the sounds of speech arriving at the baby's ears will not be loud enough to provide the basis for learning unless some special steps are taken. One of the hazards of deafness is that the defect is not a visible one. Obvious abnormalities are readily recognized at birth or soon afterwards; even blindness reveals itself at an early stage, but loss of hearing may be undetected for a long time and this has serious consequences as far as the development of speech is concerned. Mothers very often notice something strange in the early behaviour of a baby who is deaf, especially if they have already had a child with normal hearing. One mother, for example, realized that her baby was deaf at the age of twenty-seven days because it did not react in the way an elder sister had done, but usually it takes much longer than this before anyone even suspects that a baby's hearing is not normal.

Discovering at the earliest possible moment if a child has a hearing loss is vitally important for speech, for a number of reasons. For the ordinary person the word 'deaf' tends to have an all-or-none character; if you are deaf you cannot hear anything and if you are not, you can hear everything. The true state of affairs is not this at all and this is why those who are professionally concerned in the matter tend to talk more about hearing loss than about deafness. Let us go back for a moment to some of the acoustic facts that we were discussing earlier. If you are sitting about three feet away from someone who is talking in an ordinary tone of voice, the sounds are reaching you at a level of about 60 db. and they will be loud enough for you to carry on a conversation quite comfortably. You might, however, happen to be slightly deaf so that the sounds were considerably fainter, let us say about as loud as if they reached you at a level of 40 db. In that case your hearing loss for speech is 20 db. If you were much deafer than this, the sounds of speech might be quite inaudible to you even at three feet and then your hearing loss for speech is at least 60 db. and may be more. Deafness is therefore a graded effect which can be measured in decibels and most commonly the degree of hearing loss varies with frequency, that is to say a person may be particularly deaf to high frequencies, to mid-frequencies or to low frequencies, or he may be more or less equally deaf all over the frequency range. A baby who is born with a hearing loss may have any degree of loss and in any part of the range. One fact that is not generally appreciated is that it is very rare indeed for a child to be born without any capacity at all for perceiving sound; in practically every case, if enough acoustic energy is supplied to the ears, the child will experience some sensation of sound, if only within a narrow band of frequencies.

The sounds of speech as they leave the speaker's lips will not provide enough energy to be of use to a baby with a considerable hearing loss but this energy can be magnified and brought up to a useful level by means of amplifiers in the form of hearing-aids. These devices may have a number of very sophisticated features but their essential purpose is to magnify the intensity of any sounds which they transmit and so to compensate as far as possible for a hearing loss. In order that speech may develop naturally in a deaf child it is important that suitable amplification should be provided during the first year of life. It is an interesting fact that while everyone understands the need for supplying prostheses to, say, a thalidomide baby at the earliest possible stage, it is very difficult even for those closely concerned to see the importance of fitting hearing-aids to a deaf baby. The matter is of course bound up with the early detection of a hearing loss, which must be ultimately the task of a suitable clinic, but once the presence of deafness is established or even strongly suspected, it is perfectly possible for a baby of eight or nine months to be equipped with hearing-aids.

The reason why this is so important will be clear from all that has been said about the development of speech. It is a well-established fact that deaf babies babble just like hearing babies and the sounds they produce are not noticeably different. A critical moment comes, however, when in the ordinary way the sound of adult speech would act as a trigger for the child's babbling. Time after time it is reported by mothers that a deaf baby babbled up to a certain time and that then the babbling faded; this is because the sound of other people's speech is just not audible or not audible enough to the baby to continue the normal process of development. One thing that contributes to the breakdown is the fact that it is just about this time that a child begins to crawl so that it tends to move farther away from its mother. While it is in the mother's arms or on her knee a good deal of the time, her voice may be audible despite the baby's hearing loss, but when it becomes mobile, the added distance reduces the loudness of the voice. The deaf child who is fitted with hearing-aids continues to hear his mother's speech and there is a good chance that his progress will follow that of the hearing child at this vital point. There are literally hundreds of children with a severe hearing loss which has been discovered early who have acquired speech that is very little different from that of hearing people. This is because the mother in each case has realized the nature of the problem and has taken the necessary steps to see that the child was continually hearing speech despite his deafness. In more than one case this has been done in the early stages without any hearing-aids simply by the mother's talking all the time right into the child's ear. One of the most tragic things that can happen, and it still does so all too frequently, is that the mother is told either 'We cannot be sure whether your child is deaf, so please bring him back in two or three years' time and then we may be able to tell you' or else 'I am sorry to tell you that your child is very deaf, so it will not be much good trying to talk to him'. But the first months and years are of vital consequence for the acquiring of speech and language and the plain fact is that even a child with perfectly normal hearing would not learn to talk if he did not hear speech all the time. A child with a hearing loss needs to hear speech much more than a hearing child and not less; his mother needs to accompany every action and every event with speech so that the baby's brain may have the best chance of developing for itself the immense store of information which we have seen to be necessary. This is a tremendous task for any mother but if it is successfully accomplished, it is a very rewarding one since it reduces dramatically the handicap under which the child labours for the rest of its life.

It is perhaps not easy to see how, even when these steps are taken, the child can possibly work anything like normally with speech. His deafness not only makes the sounds of speech faint or inaudible, it also distorts them because it changes the relations of high, middle and low frequencies. Even with the best of hearing-aids, the deaf ear cannot hear speech as the normal ear hears it. The clue is to be found in the functioning of acoustic cues. Each individual brain evolves for itself a system of cues which works for all the distinctions that have to be made. In doing so it is in any case relying on the entirely private version of speech sounds which the ears are relaying to the brain. There is no reason at all why English listeners should all use the same acoustic cues and we can be pretty sure that they do not. What is necessary is that, whatever cues they use in a given case, they should come out with the right answer, that is to say they should recognize correctly what phoneme is represented in the string. The deaf child can do exactly the same thing provided he hears speech loud enough and often enough. His ears are supplying him with different acoustic information and with less information than normal ears, but his brain will use this to arrive at cues which work. Let us take the example of the difference between /s/ and /sh/ in English which for most of us depends on a higher pitched and a lower pitched noise. To many deaf ears these actual noises must be indistinguishable, but we noticed that the sounds are accompanied by different formant transitions and these provide a cue which is available even to most deaf ears, as long as speech is made audible. It is again the parallel of the colour blind person who judges traffic lights by their position and not by their colour. Once the whole system is established, the deaf listener may have to rely somewhat more heavily on redundancy than the normally hearing person, just as we do when there is distortion in the communication channel, and as far as his own speech is concerned, he will like the rest of us apply his acoustic cues to his own speech production, shaping his own sounds to the best of his ability until they make a match with those he hears from other people.

None of this should be taken to mean that deafness of any degree is other than a very grave disability when it is present at birth or very soon afterwards. It is a fact, however, that if deafness is discovered early enough, if proper advice is available and suitable hearing-aids are fitted and if the parents, especially the mother, are able to apply themselves to the arduous task involved, it is possible to go a very long way towards overcoming the obstacle which deafness presents to the normal acquisition of speech and language.

The principle that reception precedes production in speech is well illustrated by the case of deafness, which interferes with speech reception and may therefore prevent both reception and production. Speech production is an all-important factor in our judgment of people. Although no very high level of intelligence is needed to learn and practice the mechanics of speech, we do rely almost entirely on what people say for our judgment of their intelligence. The majority of intelligence tests are verbal tests, though in the educational world people are now careful to apply non-verbal tests as well to children whose capacity they want to assess. Too often the first judgment about a child who cannot talk to you is that he is not intelligent enough to do so and there have been many congenitally deaf children who have been classed as educationally sub-normal. The child with a hearing loss can acquire speech, as we have seen, but there are other conditions brought about by damage to the brain at birth or by congenital defects of the central nervous system which make it difficult or impossible for the child ever to achieve the controlled movements of normal speech. In a proportion of these cases mental capacity is below normal but this is not demonstrated simply by the absence of speech. A child who is severely spastic will not have the normal degree of control over voluntary movements and in extreme cases may be incapable of anything more than some minimal movement like that of a big toe or a finger or a controlled eye-blink. He will therefore never be able to make the complex movements of speech, but if he has normal hearing and is ordinarily intelligent he will learn to understand speech perfectly normally, provided of course he is given the chance by being talked to all the time. Again like some deaf children he runs the risk of being left to perish mentally, the victim of the prejudices of our talk-based society. Recent advances in technology have made it possible to provide for some people in this condition a prosthesis in the form of an electrically operated typewriter which can be worked by coded movements of a toe, a finger, the head or something of the sort, and which affords them a way of communicating with us, for this is the link in the chain which has been missing. Some truly astonishing cases have come to light as a result. One is that of a young man who is so spastic that his only controlled movements are those of his big toes and the sounds he makes are quite inarticulate. His mother was always convinced by the look in his eyes that he was quite intelligent and she took great pains to talk to him continually when he was a baby and later taught him to read, that is to say she was satisfied by the only signs she could see that he had learned to read. Repeatedly over the years she made application to those professionally qualified to know in order to find out whether there was not some kind of training that he could be given to supply him with a useful occupation but in every case she was assured that he was mentally sub-normal and could not be educated. His mother remained convinced that this was not the case and when prostheses began to be devised for those in his condition, he was accepted as a suitable recipient. Then the seeming miracle took place: he learned in no time at all to work the machine by means of toe movements and the first thing he did was to type a letter to his mother which was faultlessly typed and impeccable in spelling, in grammar, in vocabulary and in style. His abilities far exceeded anything that even his mother had ever imagined but they would have remained entirely private to him had not this method been invented of enabling him to communicate with other people. The continuation of the story is worth relating: he soon discovered that he had more than ordinary aptitude for computer programming and now leads a full, busy and useful life as a free-lance computer programmer, doing the work at home with the aid of his electric typewriter and his principal hobby is being a radio ham, for which he does all the brain work, though of course other people have to undertake the hand work.

This is in many respects a cautionary tale for it shows how much store we set by verbalization and how hypnotized we are by speech production. It also demonstrates the truth of the principle that speech reception is the primary factor in speech, since here is someone who takes in speech perfectly yet cannot produce speech at all. He operates with the normal English system of phonemes, for otherwise he would not be able to decode words correctly, although he cannot translate the phonemes into terms of articulation. It is important that the principle of recognition first should be more widely understood so that disabilities which interfere with speech production should not be automatically assumed to preclude the learning of speech reception and all that follows from it in the way of language information.

A picture of a very different kind is presented by the autistic child for in him all the necessary mechanisms are intact for both speech reception and speech production and interference with speech arises at a level which is generally considered to be psychological. The causes of autism are anything but clear and the patterns of behaviour it produces are quite varied but in general the child finds himself compelled to inhabit an almost entirely private world, cut off as far as possible from his surroundings, avoiding contact with other children and with adults and occupying himself with endless repetition of some stereotyped pieces of behaviour, related possibly to particular objects or situations. It will be at once obvious that this condition will not lead to normal speech activity since the whole purpose of speech is to operate on and to interact with the external world. In the most extreme cases the autistic child may never learn to talk, in others he may learn but will not use speech to communicate. A particular type of speech activity, for example a kind of babbling, may persist long after the time when it would disappear in a normal child and speech patterns may play a part in the stereotyped behaviour of the autistic child. An intriguing footnote is supplied by the fact that a normal baby who hears a sound recording of his own babble will make no attempt to imitate it, though it may of course trigger a fresh spate of babbling. An autistic child who hears a recording of his own pseudo-babbling is very likely to imitate it, but whether this is because he recognizes it as an element in his private world or not is far from clear.

One further speech trouble which arises in children, and one which interferes not with the learning process but with the practice of speech, is stammering. This is a difficulty which occurs in a small proportion of young children, sometimes quite early in their speech development, round about the age of three, and in other cases rather later, from about six to nine or later still. It is much more common in boys than in girls, by a factor of some three or four to one. In a number of cases it disappears after some period but it is not uncommon for the stammer to be present or potentially present through the whole of life.

The causes of stammering are on the whole rather obscure. It is generally put down to psychological factors, feelings of uncertainty and emotional unease in the child but it is often hard to be specific about the basis for stammering in an individual case. Not infrequently it appears to be associated with the emotional upset occasioned by the birth of a younger brother or sister and in such cases it is rather the parallel of the reverting to baby-talk which sometimes occurs in a toddler of three or four as a way of regaining the mother's exclusive attention. It seems fairly certain that there is a genetical component involved, that is to say that a tendency to stammer may be inherited but the trouble does not actually appear unless something in the environment triggers off the natural tendency. The popular theory that stammering is most common in left-handed children and especially in those who are made to learn to write with the right hand has never been firmly established in a statistical sense but the history of a good many individual cases certainly lends support to it. The fact that a tendency to stammer may be inherited makes it at least possible that it is associated with the inherited trait of left-handedness, particularly in the light of the growing evidence that is emerging concerning the lateralization of speech and language in the brain and the effects of mixed cerebral dominance upon the development of both speech and reading.

In the young child stammering begins simply with a tendency to repeat syllables and it is quite likely that if this stage is allowed to pass with absolutely no comment from parents or other adults the difficulty will disappear spontaneously. It is understandable that parents should be concerned when they imagine that their offspring is going to be afflicted by a stammer for the rest of his life, but the brutal truth is that the very worst forms of the disability would probably never develop were it not for the attitude and the interference of the parents or teachers. The one feature of speech that has been continually stressed throughout this book is that the working of the speech mechanism is and should be automatic. Whenever this ceases to be the case there is almost certain to be interference with speech activity. The same thing is true of all our very habitual voluntary movements; if you start to think about your movements when running down a long stairway, you are probably in for a bad fall or at the least a heart-stopping stumble; if you were compelled to give a minute running commentary on the movements of your eyes, hands, arms and legs when driving a car, you would certainly prefer to put the brakes on and come to a halt. Speech is a much more complicated set of movements than either of these and it can be carried on successfully only at the price of making the movements without paying them any attention whatsoever. When a child begins to repeat syllables, the parents' anxiety almost invariably forces them to draw the child's attention to the fact and this in itself is enough to interfere with further progress. More unfortunately still, the parents' emotion readily conveys itself to the child who in turn becomes uncertain and anxious about his own speech and in no time at all we have set up a splendidly reverberant circuit in which the child's anxiety makes it impossible for him to speak without stammering, his stammer makes the parents more anxious so that they interfere more and more with the child's speech, the stammer gets worse and the child may end up in that piteous state in which the whole speech mechanism seizes up completely at frequent intervals. This is not to say that there would be no stammerers if it were not for parental intervention, but it is certainly true that many cases would suffer less seriously and for a shorter time if their emotional involvement with the problem were not reinforced. Where the original cause of the child's uncertainty is not very deep-seated, certain types of child are able to outgrow the stammer altogether or else react to it with remarkable resilience. One is frequently struck by the attitude of many adult stammerers to their difficulty and by the nonchalance with which they accept it; it would seem that they have completely worn out for themselves any emotional involvement which they are now content to leave to their listeners.

It is difficult to infer exactly what is happening when someone stammers, even at a fairly superficial level, but it is a safe assumption that it is the feedback control of speech that is involved. We all tend to harbour some mistaken ideas about stammering, those of us that is who do not stammer ourselves. When we hear anyone saying 'ba–ba–ba–ba', we are inclined to think 'Poor fellow, he can't say a *b*', though if we come to think about it, he has just said four of them. The situation is that he cannot get on to the next part of what he has to do, which is most probably connected with the action of the larynx. Now broadly speaking, the nervous control of the larynx is a more primitive mechanism than that which controls the articulatory movements, and while normally the whole speech apparatus is under integrated control, a little further down the chain of command action has to be brought about by different nerve connections for the larynx and for the articulatory muscles. It is by no means out of the question that part of the stammerer's difficulty lies in the smooth linking together of these two controls. This would make a good deal of sense in view of the fact, which is reliably established by observation, that a stammerer's difficulties regularly disappear when he sings. In singing of even the most perfunctory sort, control is assigned predominantly to the larynx component and articulation takes a back seat, with some singers of course so far back as to be inaudible. We have already noted that the larynx is the medium for emotional expression in speech, so that by putting his larynx to work in singing, the stammerer may at the same time resolve the conflict of control between articulation and voice and reduce the emotional tension which is one cause of his difficulties.

Another aspect of control which is likely to be of some significance for stammering is auditory feedback. We have seen that delayed auditory feedback produces an artificial stammer in normal speakers and this observation has led a number of people to think that there is some connection between this phenomenon and the behaviour of the true stammerer. It must be said at once that this is very improbable on theoretical grounds and on the basis of any experiments that have been carried out. Introducing a delay into the auditory feedback loop produces a stammer. If stammerers themselves have a built-in delay, then we certainly cannot improve matters for them by adding further delay; what is necessary is that the audible signal should reach them *earlier* than it normally does. There is no way in which a speaker can hear what he says before he says it, but he can of course hear someone else say it just before he does, and this idea has given rise to the technique known as 'shadowing'. This is a method that can be very easily tried by any two speakers. One speaker begins to read aloud at a normal pace and the second speaker is instructed to repeat what the first one says, beginning as soon as he possibly can and keeping as close to him as he is able, 'shadowing' him in fact, without looking at the text which he is reading. A stammerer who is shadowing will hear the appropriate sequence of sounds in advance and this should cancel out any built-in delay in his system. When the technique was first tried, it effected a very gratifying improvement in the performance of stammerers; most of them ceased to stammer so long as they were shadowing. It was an error however to believe that the effect was dependent on shadowing, for the same stammerers performed just as well if they were made to talk with a masking noise in their ears, so that auditory feedback was simply put out of action. In the shadowing experiments, therefore, the important element was not the time interval but the fact that when the stammerer was shadowing, he was unable to hear or certainly to pay attention to the sounds of his own speech. In short one might say that a stammerer would not stammer if he did not hear himself stammer. The situation is naturally not quite as simple as that and there is no ready-made way of curing a stammer, which requires above all the liquidating of the emotional investment which the stammer represents, but if some method is adopted of giving the stammerer continual practice in speaking without stammering, this is a great step towards a final resolution of the problem.

The normal child's development of speech is marked by a succession of stages in which he is unable as yet to articulate certain sounds in the same way as the adult speakers around him. In the great majority of children such difficulties have disappeared by the age of about six or seven, but there are a few sounds which individual speakers may continue to articulate differently from their fellow speakers throughout adult life. In English the commonest perhaps is the sound representing /r/, which most of us make by curling back the tip of the tongue just behind the gums of the upper teeth. A quite sizeable minority of English speakers never learn to make the sound in this way and substitute for it a sound which is articulated by making contact between the upper front teeth and a point well back on the lower lip, rather behind the place where /v/ is made. It is a popular misconception that such speakers are replacing /r/ by /w/; this last is actually a very rare substitution except among young children. The lip–teeth version of the sound is heard a great deal in England, as an hour or two spent listening to radio or television will soon convince anyone with a reasonably acute ear. It is very prevalent among politicians and public figures of various kinds, though whether there is any association between this quirk of pronunciation and success in public life it would be hard to say.

The other frequent substitutions concern the sounds for /s/ and /z/. The true lisp, which consists in replacing these by /th/ sounds, is not really very common; all children lisp but nearly all of us grow out of it. The sound which is much more often heard is made by blowing air down the sides of the tongue in the way required for producing the Welsh *-ll-* sound. This is the sound which became so familiar through the speech of the late Winston Churchill, with his constant references during the war to the 'Nazlis'.

Such idiosyncrasies of pronunciation have no basis in organic differences between individuals but there is one case in which organic abnormality is responsible for defective articulation and that is in the child who has a cleft palate. As a result of congenital malformation, there is a split or hole in the roof of the mouth running from back to front to a greater or less extent. Sometimes, though by no means invariably, this is combined with hare lip. In many cases it is possible to carry out surgical repair of the cleft but sometimes the opening is too wide for this to be done effectively. From the account that has been given of the normal articulatory movements, it will be clear that this abnormality must affect the production of a number of sounds. For most of the time during speech, the soft palate is lifted up by the muscles attached to it so as to close off the side-branch of the vocal tract which leads out through the nose. The only exceptions occur during the articulation of nasal consonants, /m, n, ng/ in English, or of nasalized vowels in French and some other languages. A cleft in the palate means that the side branch is permanently open so that to some extent all other sounds are affected, but in certain classes of sound the effect is more noticeable. A temporary complete closure of the vocal tract is needed for the English consonants /p, t, k, b, d, g, ch, dg/ and during the closure air pressure is built up in the tract. The child with a cleft palate is unable to make the closure because air escapes all the time through the nose and prevents any build up of pressure. He is therefore not able to interpose the short silence nor to produce the burst of explosive noise that most of these sounds require by the use of the normal mechanism, though he may learn to imitate the effect by making the closure in the larynx. The whole class of hissing sounds is also affected by cleft palate because they call for a considerable increase in air flow at the point where turbulence is to be set up and again the nasal opening acts as a shunt and makes it very difficult if not impossible to get enough air flowing through the mouth to make a satisfactory sibilant. The acoustic effect of opening the passage through the nose, as we saw earlier, is to introduce an anti-resonance in the region of the second formant and this will obviously influence the quality of all sounds; the vowels in particular will sound rather nasalized. This feature together with the markedly defective articulation of the consonants just mentioned gives the characteristic quality to cleft palate speech.

We will now turn our attention to those speech disturbances which are apt to interfere with speech in adults and which are not due to the persistence of abnormalities present in childhood. As we grow older, and this means from the age of about twenty-five onwards, our hearing for high frequencies becomes less acute. In our teens we may be capable of detecting sounds with a frequency of sixteen to eighteen thousand cycles per second; at the age of sixty, we are doing very well if we can hear frequencies of eight to ten thousand cycles. These frequency ranges do not have any very great influence on the reception of speech, but in old age there is often a more rapid deterioration of hearing which leads to marked difficulties in taking in what people are saying and in particular makes the presence of background noise very troublesome. An important point is that this decline in hearing in itself does not affect the production of speech, unless of course a pathological hearing condition develops. The capital of habitual patterns of speech movement which we amass in childhood through the exercise of auditory and kinaesthetic feedback lasts us well through the ordinary span of life and a gradual modification of the sounds we hear does not interfere with these patterns. On the other hand, a sudden and traumatic onset of deafness in middle life will upset the production of speech for a variety of reasons, which include the emotional disturbance which such a misfortune is bound to occasion. In such cases complete deprivation of auditory feedback interferes with the control of speech, making it impossible to time movements and to judge the volume at which to speak and is very likely to lead to a serious deterioration in the quality of the speech. Deafness which comes on more gradually in adult life certainly affects the reception of speech, usually in one of two ways. It may interfere mainly with the transmission of sound across the middle ear mechanism and then other people's speech is simply too faint to be understood; it is like listening to a radio set which is giving out a very faint signal, even with the volume turned up to maximum. Those who suffer from this type of deafness want everyone to 'speak up' and they derive great benefit from the use of a hearing-aid. The second type of deafness also reduces the loudness of sounds that reach the ear but introduces a considerable degree of distortion as well. The result of this is that faint sounds are very faint indeed, and this applies especially to the consonants of low intensity, but loud sounds are abnormally loud and distressing. These are the people who tend to say 'Don't shout, I can hear you'; the unfortunate truth is that they can indeed hear you but they cannot understand what you say very easily because of the distortion which their deafness imposes on the incoming sounds. There are types of hearing-aid which can bring some benefit to those suffering from this type of deafness but it is very difficult to provide really adequate correction for their hearing loss. Again the effect of gradual changes in hearing upon speech production is generally not very noticeable except with regard to the volume of the speech. The person with the first type of hearing loss may well tend to speak rather softly himself because the level of his own speech in his ears is relatively high, while the second type may lead to a rather loud and penetrating voice quality which is due to the speaker's attempts to battle with the abnormally loud sounds reaching him from outside.

By far the greater part of the speech troubles which afflict people in later life, and especially in old age, are the upshot of disease or damage to the brain and central nervous system.

Since the brain is ultimately responsible for everything that happens in speech, it is inevitable that injury to the brain, however it is caused, should carry the danger of interference with speech. We have seen however that control of speech is to some degree localized, in the left hemisphere in right-handed people and in either right or left or both in left-handed people. When a person has a stroke let us say in the left half of his brain, his speech is fairly certain to be affected if he is right-handed; it may or may not be if he is left-handed. How serious the interference with speech will be depends upon the extent of the damage to the brain, as does of course the degree of paralysis which occurs at the same time.

Any and every one of the brain functions associated with speech and language is potentially at risk when the brain is damaged. The dictionary of words, with all their associations, the routines for making up sentences, the list of morphemes and phonemes, the routines for building words, the statistics of sequences at each level, the operating instructions to muscles, the feedback control loops are all elements whose working may be affected. It is most important to realize that all these functions are interlinked in an extremely complex way and that what is located in one hemisphere is the complete circuitry for dealing with speech and language. Consequently it is very unusual to find in a stroke patient that just one single aspect of speech has been interfered with. In order to illustrate the state of affairs the best analogy is probably that of the digital computer. No one who has thought at all seriously about the matter is inclined to think that the brain is 'nothing but' a digital computer, for this is manifestly not true. On the other hand, certain features of computer operation do help us to get a clearer picture of some of the things the brain is able to do, and among these is the brain's capacity for running different programs. A computer is a mass of circuitry which includes incidentally a means of storing or 'remembering' things and a means of carrying out various processes. This is all employed for a hundred and one different purposes which are specified by different programs. When a computer breaks down we cannot say, for example, that the circuits that deal with income returns have gone wrong, or those which calculate compound interest or population statistics or whatever. All these are simply programs which the computer implements. It may happen, however, that a given program demands a particular sequence of operations which the computer in its faulty state may not be able to perform accurately or perhaps at all, while another program may still run more or less satisfactorily. This is a very rough analogy with the brain circuitry that is used for speech and language. We do keep a special purpose computer in the left half of our brain which deals with speech and language, but it does so by running a variety of programs all at the same time. When the brain is damaged by accident or by a stroke, there may be several of these programs which will not run as they used to and the effects show up as a failure to deal with vocabulary, syntax, phoneme strings, speech movements and so on. When recovery takes place, as it not infrequently does, this means that other circuits have been linked into the system so that the programs can now be run again.

Given the different levels at which speech and language function, it is understandable that there should be a wide variety and different degrees of aphasia and dysphasia (total or partial loss of language function). It is usual to think of them as falling into two broad classes, those affecting speech reception and those affecting speech production, though many patients show signs of both. Memory stores such as the dictionary of words must clearly be common to both reception and production but the programs giving access to the store do not appear to be common, judging from observations of aphasic patients. Thus a patient may be in a position to recognize and to understand a great many words that are said to him but be quite unable to bring out those same words for himself when he is asked to name an object or a picture. He might for example be incapable of naming a teapot, though he could tell you that it is connected with drinking, and if you then ask him if it is a teapot, he may say 'Of course, a teapot'. The converse of this is the patient who cannot understand what is said to him or even repeat words given to him, but is able to speak spontaneously, indicating that it is the programs for decoding speech that no longer run properly.

A patient's difficulty in saying what he wants to say may show itself at different levels, other than that of word finding. In some cases the trouble lies mainly at the level of grammar and syntax so that the patient finds the words which give the content of his remark but cannot manage the grammar and so has recourse to a telegraphic style. Again he may put together successfully both the words and the grammar and have the greatest difficulty in articulating the sounds which convey the message to other people. There is often a sharp contrast between the patient who knows perfectly well what he wants to express and is frustrated by his inability to get it out and the patient who retains complete facility in speaking but cannot apply this to anything very sensible. The latter kind of patient will pour out an almost unending stream of words which does not make total gibberish but consists of repetitions of phrases and parts of words which convey nothing at all. It is noticeable that natural sounding intonations often accompany this and other kinds of dysphasic speech and it is astonishing to what lengths a patient will go in order to try to express himself. The output of one patient, for instance, was limited to repetitions of 'Sssss . . .', which seemed to be a residue of the word *yes*, and 'One, two, one, two, one, two . . .' on which he imposed a great variety of intonations and rhythms which made partial sense of his answers to questions that were put to him.

While the organization of speech and language is effected by the dominant hemisphere, there are some indications that the other half of the brain has some more primitive and rudimentary forms of speech at its disposal. Some patients who find themselves bereft of speech may in certain circumstances prove capable of cursing repeatedly and fluently, suggesting that speech for purely emotional purposes may be the function of the non-dominant hemisphere or may at least use a different program. On the other hand it may be that language material which is normally suppressed may be transferred to a special store. This would be more in line with another observation that has been made repeatedly, that people who have replaced their mother tongue by another language in later life, making some effort to suppress their first language altogether, may through brain damage lose the ability to speak the acquired language but be able to use their native language.

There are obviously a great many questions still to be answered about the interactions of brain damage and speech and these include the whole problem of recovery of speech after an injury. A very considerable proportion of stroke patients whose speech is affected do make a complete or partial recovery. This means that other circuits in the brain are pressed into service for the purposes of speech and language but how far these may be in the dominant hemisphere and how far speech functions may be taken over by the non-dominant hemisphere is not at all clear. Indeed it is true to say that we do not yet know exactly what the non-dominant hemisphere is capable of in the way of speech in the normal speaker. In the split-brain patient it is well established that the right brain cannot talk but it is more difficult to demonstrate that it cannot listen because there are some connections from the left ear direct to the left brain and therefore one cannot be sure of transmitting speech information to the right brain alone. When we consider the normal brain one added complication is that the capacity to deal with music is located in the right brain and it is hard to say what happens precisely when music and words are combined. Do the two halves of the brain work in tandem or does the right brain have its own facilities for coping with words so long as they are associated with music? The little evidence to be gained from brain damaged patients tends to favour the second possibility because one may occasionally find a patient who is totally deprived of speech and yet can sing both the tune and the words of some song which he knew before his illness.

There are a host of pathological conditions which lead to interference with speech in some degree but these are mainly of medical interest and the purpose of this brief look at what may go wrong with speech is rather to bring out those aspects which are of some importance for our understanding of speech generally. Any illness or injury that interferes with speech is bound to be distressing to the patient and it is in the nature of speech that it may well be somewhat distressing to listeners. When all is said and done, we have to recognize that, given the billions of words that are floating through the air and the millions of speakers who are talking at any one time, the incidence of any interference with speech, either temporary or prolonged, is infinitesimally small.

11

Thinking, feeling and speaking

> **Words are an aspect of the attempted communication of thought. They are not thought. When we see words described as 'thoughts', we should make sure we know this distinction.** Idries Shah

A determined effort has been made in this book to fill its pages with information about speech and to avoid discussions of theory, especially that kind of theory which bears little relation to what can be observed in real life. In this last chapter we shall be occupied with one or two questions which cannot be answered strictly on the basis of what we can see happening in speech but which are almost certainly of general interest. The working of the brain can ultimately be specified in terms of its anatomy, its electronics and its chemistry but we are very far away from being able to write any part of this specification in detail and even further from being able to give an account in these terms of what goes on when people are speaking and listening. There are many areas of human behaviour where problems cannot be tackled or questions answered directly from the viewpoint of physics or chemistry or physiology and where the only basis for discussion is that of psychology or even philosophy. Outstanding among these is the whole subject of what lies behind speech and language and of their relation to man's mental life.

An age-old question concerns the relation between thinking and speaking, or more generally between language and thought: do human beings carry on some activity which must be called thinking independently of the words in which thoughts may be couched? This question illustrates very nicely the character of such problems, which are beyond the reach of observation. The fact that any answer must itself be expressed in words merely complicates the issue. At least one fashionable philosophy of the twentieth century has replied 'No' to the question, asserting that all human thinking is constrained by the words in which the thought is expressed, that when you have explored the ways in which words are used and the syntax which governs the stringing of them together, you know what there is to be known about human thinking.

But this seems intuitively unlikely. The key to the problem probably lies in the assumption that there is one kind of thinking, whereas the experience of most of us suggests that there are different types of mental process which should be characterized in this way. There is not much doubt that a good proportion of our thinking does consist in talking to ourselves or at least in clothing our thoughts in words. A definite interaction between thought and language is apparent in the child's development and one can almost sense the step forward in thinking that takes place with some extension of language facility, for example when a child first begins to refer to himself as 'I' instead of 'me' or 'Timmy' or when prepositions like *under, over, behind, in front of* and *on top of* begin to be understood. The mental and the language processes are so bound up with each other that it does not make any sense to ask which comes first, but there is undoubtedly a kind of conceptual and operational thinking which could not develop without language practice. One experience related by Helen Keller, the totally blind and deaf girl for whom the learning of any word was a laborious and difficult business, points in this direction for she is reported as saying that it dawned on her in a flash that the word *water* stood for the stuff she drank, what she washed in and what fell when it was raining. A more general reflection of the same kind is seen in the case of a very deaf boy who had failed to achieve any communication up to the age of about twelve years and was then taught a systematic sign language in which he was able to converse. He remarked that until he had learned the sign language, his whole life had been like a silent film; he had no means of abstracting common features from experience or of conceptualizing in the way that language made possible.

It is beyond doubt then that there is a kind of thinking

which is carried on in language terms and which probably occupies much of our time. One has to know a language very thoroughly in order to think in it, however, and people who are bilingual often observe that, though they know two languages equally well, they are more inclined to think in one than in the other. One of the tests sometimes applied is to ask what language the bilingual person counts in as this may reveal that one of the two languages is more basic and more apt to act as the vehicle for thought. Language for thinking may not be restricted to our mother tongue or other natural languages we are familiar with; thinking may call upon other systems of expression. There is such a thing as mathematical thinking which makes use of mathematical expressions and operations, and this we should look upon as a language since it has its own vocabulary and its own grammar and syntax. Other people besides mathematicians almost certainly think in the languages with which they work; this is the case perhaps with the language of symbolic logic and much more commonly the various languages that have been devised for use with the digital computer, the machine language of computing and the many intermediate languages of the Fortran type.

But is this the only kind of thinking open to the human being? Surely not, unless we are convinced that all artistic pursuits for example are carried on without any thinking at all. The painter in the act of painting a canvas can scarcely be said not to be thinking but he is certainly not thinking in words nor in any system that could be called a language. Many great painters have themselves written about painting, but here we are face to face with the central difficulty of this topic, how can you make statements in words about something which does not exist in verbal form? The painter who takes up the pen is a different person from the one who wields the brush. All the same what is said in words may give a good hint about the other kind of process and one finds such hints for example in the writings of the painter Delacroix. His was an interesting example because he was intensely interested in literature and was in the habit of reading extensively as a means of stimulating his imagination and leading him to subjects which he would paint, but he seems to have been acutely aware of the switch in mental activity which the actual painting involved. He says for instance 'To imagine a composition is to combine elements one knows with others that spring from the inner being of the artist. Then from a well-stored memory forms are brought to an apparent reality'; then he says about the picture itself that its forms and colours 'even at a distance appeal to the most intimate part of the soul, transport one without words to reality by what one may call the music of the picture'. Delacroix's 'well-stored memory' was certainly not a dictionary of words and yet one could hardly say that the process by which forms were brought out of memory and transmuted into painting is not properly characterized as thinking.

The reference to 'the music of the picture' is a reminder that music itself is another sphere in which thinking must take place. It is true that there is a specific musical language which can be represented by black marks on white paper and has its own conventions and laws, but the composer does not think in this language; he makes use of it when he gets to the stage of writing down his composition so that it may become available to other people. Few composers may have had the experience of Mozart, who said that he could hear the whole of one of his symphonies in a flash from start to finish and that the only labour its composition involved was that of writing it down, but many composers have been capable of composing at enormous speed, in a sense confirming the idea that composition itself and the thinking it requires are in some measure at least independent of the formal language of music.

The example of music brings us back once more to the subject of the two hemispheres and their relation to thinking. The centre of brain activity for music is in the right half of the brain for right-handed people and other types of arts and crafts are clearly of a kind to employ the right hemisphere rather than the left. They all call for appreciation of spatial relations and for a *gestalt* view of things, even though the actual practice may involve doing one thing after another. Many occupations which are concerned with constructing and repairing mechanical and electrical devices require the right-brain style of thinking. The mechanic who is thoroughly conversant with the working of a motor-car engine cannot think out what he has to do in words nor does he even arrange it in an explicitly logical form, but he has as it were a summary view of the machine's operation in his mind and when something goes wrong, he is able to work towards this pattern by sequential steps when necessary. Any doubt about this principle may be quickly dispelled by reading almost any set of printed instructions dealing with machines, whether installing, operating or repairing them. The essence of these jobs is an appreciation of spatial inter-relations in three dimensions and a grasp of spatial cause and effect; when the attempt is made to translate these elements into words placed end to end, even with the addition of two-dimensional diagrams, the result is very often unusable and the task of making this information assimilable by the right hemisphere is so frustrating that many people give up. The best method of getting the information in seems to be to by-pass the printed word altogether and to watch someone who knows doing the job, which is the basis of the well-tried technique of learning by apprenticeship. To say that these ways of operating and learning do not involve thinking would be to become quite circular and to define thinking as exclusively left-brain, sequential mental activity.

It seems a great deal more sensible to consider that there are a number of different kinds of thinking of which left-brain sequential and right-brain holistic thinking are only two. A place has to be found somewhere in the scheme of things for the working of intuition, which in some individuals is particularly frequent. A common and facile interpretation of intuition is that it is in some way connected with emotion, but people who are able to make use of intuition are not much inclined to share this view. Emotion is always accompanied by a certain amount of heat whereas intuition brings nothing but light to bear on a given situation; it is in fact a kind of perception, but an unusual kind which sees many factors in the situation at the same time. It is tempting therefore to associate it with right-brain working but this is probably not justifiable.

We need to remember that the work of the left brain is not confined to language; it is doing a thousand other things as well and it is very likely to have its own brand of intuition which may work a little differently from the intuition of the right brain. In either case it is a form of mental activity and as such qualifies to be regarded as a form of thinking.

The balance of the evidence appears to be therefore that a good deal of our thinking is closely connected with our use of language and is actually carried out in words, but that we use other forms of thinking which are not constrained in this way and are essentially different in character. When we are in the act of talking or of listening to speech, we are always carrying on thinking of a kind though it may be a very low level style of mental activity. The experience of listening to someone 'with half an ear' is familiar to us all and, on the production side, just how slight a degree of mental supervision will suffice to keep speech going will be clear to anyone who has ever performed from memory something involving words. In these circumstances one can easily speak and 'think of something else', even though this introduces the risk of missing a cue.

Thinking and speaking are very much intertwined and our thoughts do get into our speech, but how far is this true also of our feelings? We have a variety of ways of expressing our emotions through our behaviour, by bodily movements, by gesture, by facial expression and by speech as well. There is no level of speech production that may not act as a vehicle for emotion. The comparatively primitive mechanism of the larynx we have already noted as being subject to the influence of emotion since it determines the voice quality we use. With different emotions our voice quality changes whether we like it or not and as listeners we are extremely skilled in detecting and appreciating the nuances of feeling conveyed by tone of voice. The intonation of what we say, also mediated by the larynx, is influenced by emotion, but the range of pitch we use is decided rather by the degree than by the particular nature of the emotion. But our feelings get into our speech at a much higher level than that of the larynx for our choice of words is inevitably dictated in part by this factor. There is a whole range of words which we are not much inclined to use unless we are under the stress of some fairly strong emotion, and these are not necessarily spelt with four letters. Pet names, expressions of affection, insulting and pejorative words all play their part in providing an outlet for our feelings in speech. Indeed the form of our remarks too is subject to the same pressure since strong emotion will force from us an exclamation where in cooler moments a simple assertion would fill the bill. Obviously individuals and even nations differ in the extent to which they tend to give expression to their emotions in speech. It is still the case that no Englishman can hear two members of a Latin race conversing without being persuaded that they are quarrelling violently. The contrast between the Americans and the British in this respect was once neatly summed up by an American who said that in circumstances where an American would exclaim 'Why, you damned liar!', a Britisher would say 'I hardly think so'.

We generally have the impression that we talk to a person because we want to tell him something or to ask him something, to pass on information or to get it and we may be aware often enough that our intention is to let him know how we feel about some matter or other, curiously referred to as 'giving him a piece of my mind'. What we fail to realize is that a good deal of the time, whatever our intentions may be, our speech is simply expressing our emotions; this rather than communication has become its main function. One has only to lend an attentive ear to the exchanges that go on in the course of business or family life to perceive that much of what is said would not be said at all if the only purpose of speech were communication. A superficially innocent form of words such as 'Why did you do that?' nine times out of ten is uttered only to express irritation, especially if it comes out in the form 'What did you do that for?' and the same thing is true of almost any remark that begins 'Can't you see . . .?'. Here again the expressive element relies for its outlet mainly on tone of voice and intonation but these examples show that certain sentence forms tend to become rather specialized in their function. One of the rather surprising things is that we are all very expert in recognizing the expressive element in other people's speech but most of the time we remain quite unaware how large a part it plays in our own. There may be nothing particularly harmful about expressing emotion, indeed the current fashion is more in the direction of believing that harm comes from repressing it, but what is certain is that no good can come from believing that our aim is to impart something to other people when it is actually to release some tension in ourselves.

Somewhat in contrast to this self-centred, expressive function of speech is its use for purely social purposes. Communication is itself a social business but speech performs other functions as well, one of which is that of a social lubricant. Certain individuals profess to and may themselves in fact disdain this use of speech. These are the people who are very forthright, who have no use for social graces, who pride themselves on calling a spade a spade if not a bloody shovel, who talk only when they have something to say, who always say what they mean, and who, if you observe their speech closely, will be found to make more use than anyone else of the purely expressive qualities of speech. Such people have entirely failed to digest one of the most important facts about human beings and that is that we all without exception need a certain amount of attention from other human beings. If we are deprived by circumstances of this minimum of attention, we become sick in some way or other. It is beginning to be realized that much of the delinquency occurring in modern societies is to be attributed mainly to this cause, though it has not yet quite sunk in that the organizing of children into very large schools has the inevitable effect of reducing the amount of purely human attention that an individual child can count on, in many cases to a level well below the minimum needed to keep a human being healthy.

Speech plays a key role in the exchange of this necessary attention. The various forms of greeting, the enquiries about health and family, the English chat about the weather are not the waste of time which some people consider them to be but are an absolutely necessary feature of human life, for they are the means by which we signal to each other our awareness that 'no man is an island', that we are members of a common race and that we need each other. At the lowest, biological level it is the equivalent of the grooming that goes on between animals in a group and is essential to their well-being as it is to ours. Without it, individuals begin to mope and fade or turn violently against the group, in the human case with unpleasant, even disastrous consequences. So long as we need this attention from each other, speech of this apparently rather empty kind must continue to play a vital part in the life of *homo loquens*.

The whole of humanity is an organism in which each individual is a cell. The paradox of the gift of speech is that it is at the same time the means by which we become aware of the existence of the other cells and the source of our illusion of independent existence and individuality. Among fairy tales throughout the ages and all over the world an oft repeated theme is that of the person who is allowed three gifts and who finds through bitter experience that every gift has its positive and its negative consequences. *Homo loquens* has received the gift of speech which marks him off from all other creatures that we know about and is undoubtedly responsible for his development up to the point which he has now reached. But he has had to pay for this a price which has become increasingly obvious in the modern world. Speech is the principal medium for indoctrination and conditioning, which take their most sinister forms in political ideologies and in brainwashing and are only slightly less harmful, if not so lethal, when they assume the universal power of advertising. We have become a trigger-happy society in which the trigger is not a tongue of metal or an electronic switch but a word. The pen is mightier than the sword but the slogan or political catch-phrase is mightier than either and their use has gone far towards sapping man's appetite for facts as distinct from opinions. But we have to place in the other side of the balance the fact that nearly everything we have learned as individuals, as societies and as a race has reached us in the form of traditions, stories and histories which have been passed on by word of mouth or in literature, which is speech written down. The great trouble today is that we tend to live on the 'duck soup' which figures in the tale told of the Mulla Nasrudin, the folk-hero of the Middle East, which has been published in the following translation by Idries Shah:

> A kinsman came to see Nasrudin from the country, and brought a duck. Nasrudin was grateful, had the bird cooked and shared it with his guest.
>
> Presently another visitor arrived. He was a friend, as he said, 'of the man who gave you the duck'. Nasrudin fed him as well.
>
> This happened several times. Nasrudin's home had become like a restaurant for out-of-town visitors. Every-one was a friend at some removes of the original donor of the duck.
>
> Finally Nasrudin was exasperated. One day there was a knock at the door and a stranger appeared. 'I am the friend of the friend of the friend of the man who brought you the duck from the country,' he said.
>
> 'Come in,' said Nasrudin.
>
> They seated themselves at the table, and Nasrudin asked his wife to bring the soup.
>
> When the guest tasted it, it seemed to be nothing more than warm water. 'What sort of soup is this?' he asked the Mulla.
>
> 'That', said Nasrudin, 'is the soup of the soup of the soup of the duck.'

The pressing need of the present time seems to be to get back to the duck, to rediscover that experience is the primary means of learning anything, but of course without abandoning the advantages which speech and language have brought. Without words and books *homo loquens* would never have got anywhere at all but this does not mean that we have to be eternally content with duck soup. We can learn a great deal from the man who climbs Everest and gives us a first-hand account of his experiences, for this can lead us to our own experiences of another kind, even if we never climb anything higher than Leith Hill, but when the account reaches us at twenty removes it is probably not even good entertainment. The power of speech places no barriers to the progress of man except those of his own erecting. In any case we are not going to get rid of this part of our heritage short of some cosmic catastrophe, so it behoves us to take stock and to try to see how we can minimize the drawbacks that have accumulated around our facility for verbalizing and to discover in what directions there may lie possibilities of progress for *homo loquens* – towards what, who can tell, but almost certainly to a condition where he knows more and speaks less.

Further reading

The Articulate Mammal Jean Aitchison Hutchinson: London

The Bases of Speech G. W. Gray and C. M. Wise Harper Bros.: New York

The Deaf Child Edith Whetnall and D. B. Fry Heinemann Medical Books: London

General Linguistics: An Introductory Survey R. H. Robins Longmans: London

Infant Speech M. M. Lewis Routledge & Kegan Paul: London

Intonation of Colloquial English J. D. O'Connor and G. F. Arnold Longmans: London

An Introduction to the Pronunciation of English A. C. Gimson Edward Arnold: London

Language and Communication G. A. Miller McGraw Hill: New York

Learning to Hear Edith Whetnall and D. B. Fry Heinemann: London

Linguistics David Crystal Penguin: Harmondsworth

New Horizons in Linguistics Ed. John Lyons Penguin: Harmondsworth

Phonetics J. D. O'Connor Penguin: Harmondsworth

Science and Music James Jeans Cambridge University Press: Cambridge

The Speech Chain P. B. Denes and E. N. Pinson Bell Telephone Laboratories: New York

Speech Disorders Lord Brain Butterworths: London

Index